SEAFIRE

FROM THE COCKPIT, No 13

ERIC BROWN

PUBLICATIONS

Contents

INTRODUCTION *Captain Eric Brown* CBE DSC AFC 4

BEGINNINGS *Captain Eric Brown* CBE DSC AFC 6

TESTING TIMES *Captain Eric Brown* CBE DSC AFC 14

MORE ROAR *Captain Eric Brown* CBE DSC AFC 30

CONTRA-PROP *Captain Eric Brown* CBE DSC AFC 38

MORE FROM THE COCKPIT 50

   Exaggerating the Drop *Commander Geoffrey Higgs* AFC 50

   The Defining Moment *Commander Graeme Rowan-Thomson* 52

   Big Trouble *Sub-Lieutenant Bernard Pike* 53

   Speed Trial *Lieutenant-Commander Tom Leece* 57

SEAFIRE AT WAR—1 *Rear-Admiral Ray Rawbone* CB AFC 58

SEAFIRE AT WAR—2 *Commander Tommy Handley* MiD 82

FRONT-LINE SEAFIRE SQUADRONS *Captain Eric Brown* CBE DSC AFC 94

RNVR SEAFIRE SQUADRONS 116

SECOND-LINE SEAFIRE SQUADRONS 122

SEAFIRE COLOURS 129

Flown by the Author 132

Below: Two Seafire L.IICs and a Fairey Swordfish II of 834 Squadron prepare to take off from the escort carrier HMS *Battler* in late 1943 or early 1944. During the war, a small number of front-line Fleet Air Arm squadrons were 'composite' in that they operated these two distinct types of aircraft, the Swordfish in the anti-shipping rôle and a Seafire flight for fighter protection.

INTRODUCTION

Captain Eric Brown CBE DSC AFC

THE venue was Royal Naval Air Station Yeovilton, the time was a drably grey and blustery winter's afternoon more than half a century ago and the event was the disbanding of a Royal Navy fighter squadron. The brief ceremony held at that Somerset airfield on the afternoon of 23 November 1954 did not mark *solely* the dissolution of 764 Squadron after a mere eighteen months of existence as a training unit; it signified the closing of the final chapter of a saga that had opened more than a dozen years earlier, when the war at sea was at its nadir insofar as the Allies were concerned, for 764 had enjoyed the distinction of flying the last Supermarine Seafires serving with the Royal Navy.

The Seafire, certainly aesthetically the most elegant fighter ever to grace a carrier deck, was the product of adversity; it might be said to have been born of desperation. The rôle of naval air power was expanding with the course of the war, but its full potential could not be exploited without a shipboard fighter capable of a performance at least comparable with that of contemporary enemy shore-based fighters by which it was likely to be opposed. So far as the Royal Navy was concerned, the Grumman Wildcat was placing the service's carrier-borne fighter element back in business, but, outstanding naval fighter though this purpose-built and rugged American product undoubtedly was, it lacked the performance necessary to take on the shore-based opposition on equal terms.

As a result of a brilliant piece of improvisation, the Navy had been presented with the Sea Hurricane, which had proved that a high-performance shore-based fighter *could* be operated with relative safety from a carrier, but the Hawker fighter's chances of survival against a Bf 109G or FW 190 were anything but good. Nevertheless, its successful adaptation for the shipboard rôle had at least brought about something of a revolution in naval thinking, and, logically enough, in 1941, the Admiralty began to demand a similar adaptation of what was then the highest performing fighter available—the Spitfire.

This scheme was received with mixed feelings by those naval pilots in the know. Everyone admired the Spitfire and itched to fly it—but from an aircraft

Main image: A Seafire L. Mk IIC aborting an approach for a carrier landing, having been waved off by the batsman (whose screen can be seen immediately below the port wing tip of the aircraft). The faired A-frame arrester hook of the early Seafires is clearly seen.
Above: The ultimate Seafire was the F. Mk 47, which entered service with the Fleet Air Arm well after World War II had ended. Here the pilot of a trials aircraft demonstrates a flawless carrier landing.

carrier? That was a horse of a very different colour! None needed convincing of the performance or handling attributes of this magnificent fighter, which was, surely, one of the greatest warplanes ever conceived, but there was a certain air of fragility about the aeroplane, a ballerina-like delicacy that seemed inconsistent with the demanding, muscle-taxing scenario of shipboard operations. Could that slender fuselage stand the harsh deceleration of an arrested landing? Would that frail undercarriage absorb the shock of a fifteen-feet-per-second vertical velocity, and could those wafer-like wings take the acceleration forces of a catapult launch? What of the Spitfire's high landing speed? Above all, would the pilot ever be able to see the carrier deck on the approach?

BEGINNINGS

Captain Eric Brown CBE DSC AFC

THERE were many technical difficulties, but the feasibility or otherwise of adapting the Spitfire to operate from aircraft carriers was only to be determined by practical trials and, accordingly, having obtained the somewhat reluctant agreement of the Air Ministry for the transfer of a number of Spitfires, both existing and to be produced, the Admiralty initiated late in 1941 preliminary trials with a Spitfire VB (AB205). An A-frame arrester hook had been introduced on the centre longerons aft of the firewall and at the rear of the cockpit.

The task of carrying out the trials was assigned to Lieutenant-Commander H. P. Bramwell, CO of the Service Trials Unit at RNAS Arbroath, who, after spending two weeks practising ADDLs (Aerodrome Dummy Deck Landings), took his 'hooked' Spitfire aboard HMS *Illustrious* in the Clyde during Christmas week of 1941. Peter Bramwell made twelve successful deck landings, seven take-offs and four catapult launches. Generally satisfied with the results, he did have reservations, however, and, as little of the deck could be seen during a normal straight final approach, he recommended that a curving approach technique be adopted so that the pilot could keep the batsman (Deck Landing Control Officer) in sight for as long as possible. He also expressed some doubt as to the Spitfire's suitability for operation from US-built 'Woolworth' escort carriers.

His report was sufficiently encouraging to warrant Admiralty confirmation of a programme covering the transfer and adaptation of 250 Spitfires for naval use. It was proposed that these would comprise 48 existing Spitfire Mk VBs with the remainder being new-production Mk VCs, and, as the name 'Sea Spitfire' was somewhat dissonant, the contraction

'Seafire' was officially adopted for the 'hooked' Spitfire. Adaptation for shipboard use was to be the essence of simplicity, and, apart from changes to internal equipment such as the introduction of naval HF R/T and IFF and a homing beacon receiver, was to comprise the provision of a hydraulically damped and faired A-frame arrester hook released by means of a Bowden cable, and slinging points, with the necessary local strengthening. The reworking of the Spitfire Mk VBs was undertaken by Air Service

Main image and above: The early Seafires were conversions of Spitfire Mk VBs and differed only in having arrester hooks and slinging points and incorporating minor modifications to communications equipment. BL676 was the first Seafire to be converted to this specification—as opposed to being merely a 'hooked' Spitfire; designated Mk IB, it retained the Vokes tropical sand filter beneath the nose that was originally designed for RAF aircraft operating in the Western Desert. It retained the Dark Green and Ocean Grey disruptive camouflage applicable to RAF day fighters of the time and bore the legend 'Bondowoso' (marking it as a presentation aircraft from the district in southern Java of that name) either side of the fuselage just ahead of the windscreen.

Training Ltd as Seafire Mk IBs, but these were intended for use as trainers and they lacked the slinging points and homing beacon receiver which were introduced on a further 166 Seafire Mk IBs that were later to be delivered to the Navy by both Air Service Training and Cunliffe-Owen Aircraft.

The Seafire Mk IB was viewed as an interim model with which squadrons would be enabled to work up pending delivery of the assembly line adaptations of the new-production Spitfire Mk VCs which had been assigned the designation Seafire Mk IIC, but, owing to alacrity on the part of Supermarine in delivering Seafire Mk IICs, the first example of each version reached the Navy on the same day, 15 June 1942. The Seafire Mk IC differed from the Mk IB essentially in having the universal or 'C' wing—although the extra pair of 20mm cannon that could be accommodated by this wing was never to be fitted in service as the weight penalty was to be found unacceptable—and catapult spools, the spigots for which called for some local beefing up. Some further strengthening was provided by an external fish plate between the forward cockpit bulkhead and the radio bay, the CG change resulting from the new installations and strengthening being restored by balance weights.

My first acquaintance with the Seafire was made in August 1942, when I was serving with 897 Squadron at RNAS Stretton. At that time we were operating Fulmars, and I was somewhat puzzled at being instructed to proceed to Donibristle to bring back two Seafire Mk IBs which were then allocated to me to build up some experience. At the beginning of September, I was abruptly sent off to RNAS Machrihanish in a Hurricane, which was exchanged for a Wildcat upon my arrival. After a fifteen-minute refamiliarisation flight in the Wildcat the next morning, I was sent off to the escort carrier HMS *Biter* for a series of deck landings and catapult launches, ostensibly to proof the ship's catapult. On returning to Stretton, I found myself a member of 801 Squadron, which had re-formed on 7 September with a complement of a dozen Seafire Mk IBs and was, in fact, destined to be the only operational FAA squadron to be fully equipped with this mark. At Stretton, the object of all my to-ing and fro-ing was finally revealed to me: I had been selected to undertake the first Seafire deck trials on an escort carrier!

Opposite page: BL687 was the second 'full' Seafire conversion and is shown with its tail trestled to demonstrate the arrester hook. The paintwork, clearly only recently applied, has a noticeably matt finish.
Above: BL676 again, here in port profile, with the windscreen framing and main canopy framework evidently yet to be painted. The slinging points required for 'navalised' Spitfires are clearly seen immediately behind the main removable port engine panel and just forward of the fuselage roundel. BL676 conducted the type's first deck-landing trials on board the fleet carrier HMS Illustrious on 8 May 1942.
Below: BL676 conducted further carrier-compatibility trials on board HMS Victorious shortly afterwards; the aircraft is shown here—evidently having been repainted and also having shed its tropical intake since it was first revealed—during a take-off run from the carrier. Such was the secrecy required during wartime that this photograph was not released for publication until December 1942, some six months after it was taken. BL676 was re-serialled MB328 at some stage—conceivably just prior to these trials during the general re-finishing.

It was back to Machrihanish again, and at 1330 hours on 11 September I was flying a Seafire towards HMS *Biter*—the time being significant, as it turned out. As I approached *Biter*, I confidently assumed that all would be breached up for this momentous occasion—the first landing of a Seafire on one of these postage stamp-sized platforms—and I did a quick circuit at 400 feet and settled into my approach. Contrary to Peter Bramwell's earlier recommendations, I adopted a straight final approach with the aircraft crabbed to starboard so that I had a good clear view to port of both the deck and, supposedly, the batsman, of whom, in the event, I saw no sign. Nevertheless, all went smoothly and I touched down on *Biter*, picking up the second wire. I came to a stop somewhat smartly and cut the engine, and it was only then that I realised that the deck was completely deserted! Then striding from the island came a lone figure—the Captain. He stepped up on the wing and said, with a pleasant smile, 'I say, old boy, you were not expected so early and everyone's at lunch!' It was only then that the truth dawned on me: I had landed with the carrier 25 degrees out of wind, only thirteen knots of wind speed over the deck, the arrester wires lying flat and unsupported, and no batsman!

Since the programme called for me to start with 32 knots of wind and work down to 20 knots, I felt that, albeit inadvertently, I had proved something. The Captain agreed that much of the programme could be taken as read and forthwith sent a signal to the Admiralty announcing successful completion of the trials! Perhaps this was a little premature as, after lunch, it was decided that I should make a landing with 10–12 knots wind over the deck. With the help of the batsman, the landing was perfectly straightforward, but as the arrester wire reached the end of its pull-out my arrester hook parted company with my aircraft. Since no crash barrier was being used for the trials and it was obvious that my brakes would not prevent me trickling over the bows and being run over by the carrier, I swung the Seafire gently into the island, bringing it to an abrupt halt with surprisingly little damage.

I was, of course, totally unaware at the time that the panic to get a Seafire aboard an escort carrier was a part of the preparation for Operation 'Torch', the Allied invasion of North Africa that was to commence in the early hours of 8 November, two months later. As it turned out, the three escort carriers involved, *Biter*, *Dasher* and *Avenger*, were all to be armed with Sea Hurricanes for this assault, the Seafires operating primarily from the elderly carriers *Argus* and *Furious*, which had T-shaped elevators capable of accommodating the non-folding fighters, while the more modern *Formidable* and *Victorious*, with lifts too small to accept these early Seafires, were each to stow a half-dozen of the fighters in permanent deck parks where they were exposed to the elements.

Left and below: Pilots of 807 Squadron and flight-deck handlers get to know their new Seafire Mk IICs on board HMS *Furious*, August 1942. It would not be long before the Seafire aircrews would see action, in Operation 'Torch', the Allied invasion of North Africa in November that year.
Above: The Seafire Mk IIC quickly followed the Mk IB. Adapted from the Spitfire VC, it employed the 'Universal' or 'C' wing: two 20mm cannon were provided for in each mainplane, although in practice Seafires were fitted with only one in each, in order to save weight. Tropical filters were issued with the aircraft but, again, were rarely fitted. MA971, nearest the camera, was the first Mk IIC to be received by the Navy; it and its companions in 807 Squadron are seen here at RNAS Lee-on-Solent in June 1942 prior to joining HMS *Furious*.

The tempo at which squadrons had been converting to the Seafire had meanwhile been building up. 807 had received its first Seafire Mk IIC at Lee-on-Solent towards the end of June, and late in August, three other squadrons, 880 and 885, formerly on Sea Hurricanes, and 884, previously equipped with Fulmars, converted to Seafire Mk IICs, the last-mentioned unit at Stretton and the others at Lee, while in the following month 801 began, as previously mentioned, working up on the Seafire Mk IB. During its six weeks' work-up, 801, incidentally, succeeded in landing-on at sea all twelve of its Seafires with only 23-second intervals between aircraft.

The first of the new Seafire squadrons to embark for 'Torch' was 880, assigned to the old and slow HMS *Argus* with a complement of eighteen Mk IICs, followed a few days later by 801 with a dozen Mk IBs and No 807 with a similar number of Mk IICs, both embarked on board HMS *Furious*, while 884 and 885, with a half-dozen Seafire IICs apiece, joined the fleet carriers HMS *Victorious* and HMS *Formidable*, respectively. The first Seafire actions of 'Torch' were an unsuccessful strafing attack by 885 Squadron, which was frustrated by thick ground haze, and a sweep over the Tafaroui naval air base by 807 Squadron. While returning to *Furious*, 807 was bounced by Dewoitine 520s, Sub-Lieutenant G. C. Baldwin obtaining the first confirmed 'kill' for the Seafire (a New Zealander, Sub-Lieutenant A. S. Long of 885 Squadron, had earlier been credited with a 'probable' after attacking a Martin 167 over Mers-el-Kébir harbour). One unusual story involving a Seafire on this first day of 'Torch' concerned Sub-Lieutenant L. P. Twiss of 807 Squadron, later to become a well-known test pilot. Twiss landed alongside a US Army tank column to give warning of a hidden anti-tank battery and subsequently made two reconnaissance flights at the special request of the commander of the column. Short on fuel, he was forced to land at Tafaroui, which had still to be taken by the Allies, spent the night under the wing of his aircraft and next morning persuaded the French to refuel his Seafire and then returned to *Furious*.

Operation 'Torch' had provided the first large-scale blooding of the Seafire, and if there was some little disappointment among personnel at the lack of vigorous opposition, the début had been by consensus successful. Nevertheless, there was some concern over performance shortcomings, initial climb rate and low-altitude speed particularly leaving

Left: Personnel and a Seafire Mk IB of 801 Squadron after the 'Torch' operation. The temporary US-style national markings were, according to some sources, applied in order to aid the Americans in distinguishing friend from foe.

Right and below: In late June 1943, as part of her post-refit shake-down, HMS *Illustrious* embarked a variety of different aircraft types in order to test her new equipment, which included additional arrester wires and outriggers for parking Seafires. These two photographs date from that time and show a Seafire Mk IIC on board the carrier. In the photograph at right, the wartime censor has deleted the Type 285 'yagi' aerial (for high-angle gunnery radar) that would otherwise have been visible above the aircraft's port wing.

COURTESY DAVID HOBBS

something to be desired. The Seafire Mk IIC was some 13–15 knots slower than the Mk IB at all altitudes owing to the heavier 'C' wing and the added weight of local strengthening coupled with the greater drag of the wing, to which could be added that of the catapult spools. Prior to 'Torch', Seafire Mk IBs of 801 Squadron flying from *Furious* and participating in Operation 'Train' had failed to overhaul Ju 88s shadowing the force in which the carrier was included, and the German bomber had proved capable of outdistancing the Seafire Mk IICs of 807 Squadron with some ease.

These frustrating encounters were primarily responsible for the decision to test the Merlin 32 in the Seafire, this differing from the Merlin 45 or 46 in having a cropped supercharger impeller, maximum boost being raised to plus 18 pounds and maximum output rising by 430hp at 3,000 feet to 1,640hp, full advantage of the increase being taken by means of a four-bladed propeller which replaced the standard three-blader. With this engine change, the fighter became the Seafire L. Mk IIC and I was to become familiar with this variant when it first arrived in November 1942 at the Service Trials Unit at Arbroath, to where I had been posted on 12 September after my brief sojourn aboard *Biter*.

The Seafire L. Mk IIC was the most exciting aircraft that I had flown to that time. Its initial climb rate and acceleration were little short of magnificent, and at maximum boost it could maintain 4,600 feet a minute up to 6,000 feet. The fully supercharged Mk IIC took at least two minutes longer to attain 20,000 feet and was markedly slower at all altitudes up to 25,000 feet. Later, some Seafire L. Mk IICs were to have their wing tips clipped to boost roll rate and, incidentally, add another four knots to the maximum speed, although these advantages were to be obtained at some cost in take-off run and service ceiling. Another result of the installation of the Merlin 32 was a quite dramatic reduction in take-off distance and, in fact, the L. Mk IIC without flaps could get airborne in a shorter distance than the standard Mk IIC using full flap! My enthusiasm for this new Seafire variant was such that, one afternoon, in sheer exhilaration, I looped it around both spans of the Forth Bridge in succession—court-martial stuff nowadays, but during a war nobody has the time to bother with such formalities.

On 15 December 1942 I took the Seafire L. Mk IIC aboard HMS *Activity* and performed a series of fifteen deck-landing and take-off tests to a limit run of 360 feet, which was reached in 25 knots of wind at an all-up weight of 7,183 pounds. There was little doubt of the efficacy of the Merlin 32-engined Seafire, and as a result of these and other trials the decision was taken to convert all Merlin 46-engined Seafire Mk IICs to L. Mk IIC standard, the conversion programme commencing during the following March and the first unit selected to operate this type being 807 Squadron.

It was about this time that I witnessed a very unusual incident at Machrihanish when the airfield was alerted that a Seafire being flown by Lieutenant David Wilkinson (later to be killed in a flying accident) had a mechanic wrapped around its rear end! The mechanic, a rating appropriately enough named Overhead, had apparently been lying on the tail of the Seafire to hold it down while running up on the deck of a carrier in the Clyde area. Wilkinson had throttled back to let the mechanic off, but owing to a misunderstanding the mechanic had remained where he was and the Seafire had taken off with him clinging on for dear life. The pilot could not account for the extraordinary tail-heaviness of his Seafire until he was alerted by radio of the situation. He promptly headed for Machrihanish at low level and slow cruise, the slipstream clamping the unfortunate mechanic in position. A straight-in approach to the runway and a 'wheeler' landing to keep the tail up as long as possible, and the mechanic's ordeal was over. He had suffered shock and the effects of cold, but was otherwise totally unhurt.

TESTING TIMES

Captain Eric Brown CBE DSC AFC

THE further expansion of the Navy's Seafire component began in December 1942, when two more Fulmar squadrons, 808 and 887, converted to Mk IICs, and 880 Squadron was spilt to provide the nucleus of another squadron, 889. The equipment of these units, the provision of replacements for squadrons that had participated in 'Torch' and the establishment of adequate reserves absorbed all production—by now primarily from Westland Aircraft, which had been allocated responsibility for Merlin-engined Seafire development, with Cunliffe-Owen as the company's sub-contractor—until the spring of 1943, when a further half-dozen squadrons (809, 879, 886, 894, 895 and 897) were re-armed with the Seafire IIC. The total complement of first-line Seafire squadrons was now fourteen, giving the Seafire the distinction of being the most numerous combat aircraft type in Royal Navy operational service.

Between 29 December 1942 and 3 January 1943 I had had the task of giving Seafire deck-landing instruction to No 65 (F) (East India) Squadron RAF, and on 15 January I was again dispatched to *Activity* for a further series of fifteen deck-landings and take-offs with a Mk IIC, this time to a limit run of 370 feet reached in a 20-knot wind. In the following month, a Mk IIC equipped with RATOG (Rocket-Assisted Take-Off Gear) from RAE Farnborough carried out trials on board HMS *Illustrious* and, for comparison purposes, I joined in with an L. Mk IIC, which, as usual, took-off like a scalded cat with 175 feet in 30 knots of wind. The RATOG trials were the direct result of the fact that, other than the fleet carriers of the *Illustrious* class, the Navy's carriers did not have catapults compatible with the spigots and spools of the Seafire, rockets thus being the only readily available means of shortening take-offs. Although the trials on board *Illustrious* were pronounced successful and subsequent production Seafires were provided with RATOG attachment points, this rather dramatic means of reducing take-off distances possessed some obvious operational

Left and below: RATOG—Rocket-Assisted Take-Off Gear—was, on Seafires, a remarkably straightforward device. Each pair of rockets was located along a wing root, angled outwards and downwards to produce the required thrust line (discharging well away from the airframe), their simple containers secured to the forward slinging point and via a sprung hook on the wing itself. Jettison was accomplished by the pilot activating the forward latch, the elastic cord (visible) then pulling the device clear of the aircraft disadvantages and was never, in fact, to be used by Seafires during the war.

Soon afterwards, the Service Trials Unit moved from Arbroath to Crail on the Firth of Forth, and from here I was sent to give deck-landing instruction to Nos 411 (F) and 416 (F) Squadrons at Kenley and No 402 (F) Squadron at Digby, all Royal Canadian Air Force units. There was an incidental bonus for me at Kenley as the extroverted Canadians would only agree to a session of ADDLs if I, in turn, agreed to accompany them on a fighter sweep over France, and so a most illicit 'swap' system was initiated with me as an admittedly willing victim.

In June 1943 the Navy's latest carrier, HMS *Indomitable*, having been completed with an enlarged forward lift, embarked no fewer than forty Seafire Mk IICs and L. Mk IICs, but there was no gainsaying that the lack of wing folding had been a serious nuisance as, apart from *Argus* and *Furious*, no Royal Navy carrier had previously possessed lifts large enough to enable them to strike down their Seafires undismantled. The problem had, of course, been seen from the outset and work had been proceeding apace on providing the Seafire with a wing-fold system. At first sight, the folding of such a thin wing appeared to present virtually insoluble problems if loss of stiffness and excessive weight were to be avoided, but with commendable speed Supermarine had devised a system of two straight

Above: RATOG provided considerable temporary thrust, enabling the Seafire to take off, as the author says, 'like a scalded cat'. This photograph, of an L. Mk IIC making a RATOG-assisted getaway from the runway at Farnborough, clearly demonstrates that this is no exaggeration!

Left: The hurried 'navalisation' of the Spitfire meant that early Seafires were unable to fold their wings and, as a result, could only be struck below on board the elderly carriers *Argus* and *Furious*, which had lifts of the requisite dimensions. Even so, there was little room to spare, as this photograph of an unarmed 'hooked' Spitfire VB of 768 Squadron, taken during deck-landing training on board *Argus* in September 1943, shows. The carrier's forward lift was 36ft 2in square and the aircraft's wing span was 36ft 10in—hence manpower was required to manœuvre the aircraft into a diagonal position.

fore-and-aft folds, a break being introduced at the outer wheel well extremities from which the wing hinged upward manually, a second fold at the wing-tip joint turning downward to afford an acceptable stowage height. It was ascertained that at least 90 per cent of the 'C' wing's torsional rigidity factor could be maintained and, in the event, the weight penalty was restricted to 125 pounds.

The prototype conversion (MA970)—actually an adaptation of Supermarine's first production Seafire Mk IIC—commenced its test programme in mid-November 1942 and came to us at Crail in June 1943, barely three months before Westland was due to initiate production deliveries of the Seafire Mk III, and at the Service Trials Unit we were more concerned with its deck-handling than its flight characteristics, although I carried out one check flight with the prototype on 16 June. In fact, the production Seafire Mk III differed from preceding versions in one respect other than its folding wing: it had a Merlin 55 engine with automatic boost control and barometrically governed full-throttle height, which relieved the pilot of the need to use his judgement in order to get the most out of his engine. The Merlin 55 had the same combat rating (1,415hp at 11,000 feet) as the earlier Merlin 45 of the Mk IIC but drove a similar four-bladed propeller to that of the L. Mk IIC.

The Seafire Mk III displayed almost identical handling qualities to those of the Mk IIC but it was seventeen knots faster at all altitudes. Deliveries were to begin to 894 Squadron late in November 1943, but by that time production was already to have given place to that of the L. Mk III, this having a low-altitude Merlin 55M with a cropped supercharger impeller like that of the Merlin 32, the collector pipes being supplanted by individual exhaust stacks which both reduced weight and provided a modicum of thrust. The Seafire L. Mk III—which was to be built in larger numbers than any other Seafire variant—began to reach the squadrons in quantity during the spring of 1944.

The month of July 1943 saw further operational deployment of Seafires in support of a major Allied

Left and above: The problem of hangar stowage on board ship was solved by the introduction of the Mk III, the first Seafire to feature wing-folding. The initial wing conversion was installed on MA970, a Mk IIC, shown here. Jury struts ensured rigidity, and folding wing tips brought the overall height down to the acceptable level.
Below: LR765 was the first production Seafire Mk III and was built by Westland; however, this and other early Mk IIIs retained the three-bladed propeller associated with the Merlin 45. The use of orthochromatic film for this image has resulted in the yellow surround to the fuselage roundel appearing very dark.

assault, the newly commissioned *Indomitable* carrying what was at that time the largest fighter complement ever embarked by a Royal Navy carrier, comprising the Seafire L. Mk IICs of 807 Squadron and the Mk IICs of 880 and 899 Squadrons, intended as a major part of the fighter cover for Force 'H' mounting Operation 'Husky', the invasion of Sicily launched on 10 July. For me, the month involved intensive Seafire development flying and culminated in instructions to undertake a series of landings on escort carriers to ascertain the minimum acceptable wind speed at which a Seafire could be operated, bearing in mind (so my instructions informed me) that RAF pilots might also have to make landings with 'hooked' Spitfires and without the benefit of previous deck-landing experience.

Thus, on 3 August, I completed ten low-wind-speed landings on board HMS *Fencer* and, on 11 August, twenty similar landings on HMS *Tracker*, rounding these off on 14 August with another five landings on HMS *Pretoria Castle*, all with a Seafire Mk IB and without any untoward problems. The next month, the real purpose behind these trials emerged when Operation 'Avalanche' was mounted

Left: Seafires of 879 and 886 Squadrons prepare to take off from the escort carrier HMS *Attacker* during Operation 'Avalanche', the landing at Salerno Bay during the Allied invasion of Italy, September 1943. Each carries a 500-pound bomb on its belly rack.

Right, upper: The attrition rate for Seafires during the Salerno episode was high and was brought about principally by the numerous deck-landing accidents. Here flight-deck crews on board *Attacker* attend a Seafire following a 'prang'.

Right, lower: Seafire 'K' of 879 Squadron having has its progress rudely interrupted by the safety barrier, again on board HMS *Attacker* in September 1943.

Below: Seafires of 885 Squadron ranged and about to take off from the fleet carrier HMS *Formidable* during the 'Torch' operation, November 1942. The aircraft nearest to and furthest from the camera are Mk IBs and are fitted with Vokes filters; the other two, which have the 'C' wing, are Mk IICs. The flight-deck centreline was of limited assistance to the departing Seafire pilot as he was unable to see it from his cockpit. Notice that the ship's flight deck is painted in disruptive camouflage.

on the morning of the 9th to put Allied forces ashore in the Bay of Salerno, the bulk of the air cover being provided by Seafire L. Mk IICs from no fewer than five escort carriers, which, between them, carried nine squadrons and two flights with 106 aircraft. The carriers were *Attacker* (879 and 886 Squadrons), *Battler* (807 and 808 Squadrons), *Hunter* (899 Squadron and 834 Flight), *Stalker* (880 Squadron and 833 Flight) and *Unicorn* (809, 887 and 897 Squadrons). The weather was calm with very little wind and the escort carriers were operating at wind speeds which were virtually those created by their own speed of about 18 knots; small wonder that the Admiralty had been anxious about low-wind-speed landings. As it was, there were a large number of 'prangs' as hooks pulled out or pilots missed the wires and hurtled into crash barriers, no fewer than 42 Seafires being written off.

The unexpectedly high incidence of deck-landing accidents during the first day of 'Avalanche'—Seafire

Opposite page, top: For much of the time from 1943 the escort carrier HMS *Ravager* fulfilled the rôle of the Royal Navy's deck landing training carrier and as such was host to some spectacular Seafire incidents—as here.
Below: The safety barrier did not prevent deck-landing accidents but it normally restricted the carnage. This dramatic photograph has caught a Seafire IIC at the moment of engagement.
Above: The aftermath. The same Seafire, its undercarriage trapped, has performed a half-somersault and the safety of the pilot is being urgently addressed by the flight-deck crews. The aircraft forward, at least one of which is still manned, are unscathed.

availability dropped by something of the order of 38 per cent by the second day as a result—was largely responsible for the fact that the escort carriers had only 39 serviceable Seafires at dawn on D-Day plus Two! The problem was promptly dumped back in our laps for further solution, one result being that, on 30 September, I carried out fifteen landings into the arrester wires on the dummy deck at Arbroath while photographs were taken of each stage of each landing. These tests led to some arrester hook modifications and I was sent off on 26 November with a Seafire L. Mk IIC with strengthened hook for landing trials aboard HMS *Ravager*.

On my way to *Ravager* from Arbroath, I landed at Abbotsinch to refuel. On take-off the throttle jammed at full power, and, since Abbotsinch was in a built-up area, I headed for Ayr airfield, reaching it in four minutes flat like a bat out of hell, cutting the magneto switches and gliding in. The fault was soon cured and I resumed the flight to the carrier. I made ten landings on *Ravager*, starting at 17 knots wind speed and reducing ship's speed by one knot per landing until the propeller tips clipped the deck at a recorded retardation of 2.03g. I was flown ashore to pick up a replacement L. Mk IIC, and the next day was back on board *Ravager*. Over the course of two days, I carried out a further thirty landings at various low wind speeds and combinations of arrester-wire settings. At first, the batsman gave me three successive wave-offs so I landed anyway, and after a parley among the trials team it was decided that would be fairer to remove the batsman, who was not used to the Seafire, to my crabbed approaches, or to the fast approach speeds that we were recording.

Left, below and right: Further landing mishaps involving Merlin-engined Seafires. The aircraft's reluctance to perform textbook landings could be ascribed to its high landing speed (compared to most other naval aircraft types, the majority of which were designed specifically to naval requirements), its lengthy forward fuselage, making visibility directly ahead problematic for the pilot, and its fragile, narrow-track main undercarriage. With experience in service, most pilots were, however, able to overcome their difficulties. All four of these photographs were taken on board escort carriers, and the aircraft depicted in that at the foot of this page is of especial interest in terms of its markings. A Seafire IB converted from a Spitfire VB, it features a widely spaced, RAF-style serial number, a red and white spinner, and what appears to be a fin flash with the colours back to front and with the red area extended upwards. The aircraft is an 842 Squadron Seafire on board HMS *Fencer*—a unit known for its individuality of touch in terms of *décor*.

These trials were intended to produce answers which were required before the mounting of Operation 'Dragoon', the invasion of the South of France in which it was hoped that Seafires launched from escort carriers would once again play a major rôle. The 'Avalanche' operation had undoubtedly tarnished the Seafire's reputation and the attrition that it had suffered was totally unacceptable. Although we believed that we had resolved the hardware problems reasonably satisfactorily, the Fifth Sea Lord, Rear-Admiral D. W. Boyd, now wanted to know something of the pilot problems associated with the aircraft. He felt that I was too experienced in deck-landings to give him the answers, so he made Jeffrey Quill, the most experienced Spitfire pilot in Britain, a Lieutenant-Commander RNVR in the Fleet Air Arm and sent him deck-landing in the Seafire with a directive to report back on his findings.

Jeffrey Quill was an inspired choice as he had the analytical mind of a superb test pilot trained to find answers to any flight problems. He submitted his report on 29 February 1944, and it made four main observations: (i) pilots had to be trained to employ a curved approach to the deck as the crabbed approach was acceptable only for skilled and experienced pilots; (ii) multi-ejector type exhaust manifolds should be fitted to all Seafires and the pilots should be trained to land with their heads out of the cockpit and looking along the port side of the engine cowling; (iii) the Seafire had inherent poor speed controllability; and (iv) the Seafire lacked the necessary robustness for carrier landings, but the fitting of a 'sting' type hook would probably reduce the accident rate. This report was not entirely encouraging, and the sour reputation that the Seafire was acquiring was in no way relieved by common knowledge of the greater sturdiness, better endurance and markedly superior deck-landing and ditching qualities offered by the new Grumman Hellcat. Furthermore, the less tractable side of the Seafire's nature was prone to exaggeration and the result was that many pilots were unduly apprehensive of deck-landing this fighter.

By the time Jeffrey Quill's report was rendered, I had become Chief Naval Test Pilot at RAE Farnborough, my predecessor having been killed landing a Seafire on board a carrier at the beginning of 1944, and I was now to be heavily committed to test programmes involving the second-generation Griffon-engined developments of this shipboard fighter. However, these were to be interspersed with trials involving the earlier Merlin-engined models, such as a new series of RATOG tests with a Seafire L. Mk IIC, these being a continuation of the earlier trials at the RAE and on board *Illustrious*, and directly connected with the forthcoming Operation 'Dragoon'. For rocket-assisted take-offs it was necessary to set the elevator trimmer one division more nose-up than for normal take-off in order to counteract the nose-down thrust produced by the rockets on firing. Eighteen degrees of flap was set by getting the groundcrew to insert wedges when the flaps were down, these being held secure once the flaps were raised. The wooden wedges had been found necessary as the Seafire's flaps could be only fully lowered or fully housed and this improvisation produced a take-off setting, the wedges being discarded once the Seafire was airborne by selecting flaps down, the wedges falling away and the flaps then being fully raised. The throttle friction nut had to be screwed up tightly to counteract acceleration effect, as the firing button was depressed on the throttle handgrip. On receiving the take-off signal, the pilot turned the firing button to 'Fire', ran up

Left: A night take-off by a Seafire IIC using RATOG. The use of this device at night on carrier decks posed problems for pilots ranged behind an aircraft employing it, and these were one of the many topics addressed by the author during his time as a Seafire test pilot.
Below: Seafire IICs are manœuvred into the rain-swept deck park on board HMS *Indomitable* during Operation 'Husky', the Allied invasion of Sicily, in June 1943. The new carrier embarked some forty Seafires for the operation, but owing to the Mk IIC's non-folding wings the entire complement had to be carried topside.
Right: A Seafire L.IIC on board the escort carrier HMS *Hunter* awaits the signal to take off. Handlers stand by as 'Bats' discusses a problem with his colleagues.

fully on the brakes and applied rudder to counteract swing as the brakes were released. On drawing abeam of the firing-point flag, the firing button was depressed and the torque swing then tended to damp out. The Seafire had to be held in the three-point attitude during the entire take-off run if full benefit was to be obtained from the thrust line of the rockets. Ideally, the rockets died just after the Seafire became airborne, the undercarriage then being retracted and the expended RATOG units being jettisoned while airspeed was still low. Asymmetric rocket failures were explored and, for realism, I was not informed as to which side the rocket had been disconnected. Since the Seafire had only one rocket on each side the effect was minimal. Night take-offs were also made, and these necessitated the immediate transfer of attention to the blind-flying instruments as the rockets were fired in order to avoid risk of momentary blindness as a result of rocket glare. The pilots of aircraft on a carrier deck ranged aft of the Seafire taking off had to close their eyes for about five seconds as soon as they saw it signalled off as otherwise the flash dazzled them for quite a while.

By mid-summer of 1944 the tempo of Griffon-engined Seafire development was accelerating, but I still had occasion to fly its Merlin-engined predecessor from time to time. One of the tasks that I had enjoyed most from the outset of my tenure at the RAE was being launched in a Seafire from the twenty-foot-high rocket-powered catapult, usually to amuse (or alarm) visiting dignitaries. On 10 July I was giving such a demonstration in my trusty Seafire L. Mk IIC, which had been loaded on the heavy

SEAFIRE

TESTING TIMES

Left, upper: Two pilots chat on board HMS *Indomitable*, March 1943. The Seafire IIC—with Vokes filter—is an 899 Squadron aircraft (although the chocks are 880's!).
Left, lower: A Seafire parked alongside the catapult (accelerator) of one of the *Illustrious* class carriers, with a clear view of the shuttle that propelled the aircraft forward. On these ships, to avoid weakening the armoured flight deck the mechanism had to be mounted on top of it—thus standing proud—rather than within it.
Right: Bombing up an 899 NAS Spitfire Mk III. Notice the port for the gun camera in the wing root and the protective strip along the leading edge of the propeller blade.
Below: An 885 Squadron Seafire utilising HMS *Formidable*'s catapult. The shuttle raised the tail of the aircraft so that the latter assumed a flying attitude.

Above: The deck park on board the escort carrier HMS *Khedive*, spring/summer 1944; the aircraft are Seafire Mk IIIs and the squadron is 899 NAS. The aircraft's wing tips have already been hinged down and the jury struts are in position preparatory to wing folding.

Below: Seafire Mk IIIs, equipped with detachable 30-gallon underbelly fuel tanks, prepare for take-off as the flight-deck handlers complete their tasks. The close proximity of whirling blades and fierce draughts made such work hazardous in the extreme.

metal cradle by means of four metal spools attached to the aircraft and engaging claws on the cradle legs. After a very short run under the power of the battery of rockets attached to the bottom rear of the cradle, two long, pointed prongs on the front of the cradle theoretically engaged two tubes filled with water and sealed by fibre discs, penetration of the discs allowing the prongs to expel the water under pressure and bring the cradle to a standstill within its own length, the aircraft automatically disengaging for free flight. On this particular occasion, someone had forgotten to fill the water tubes, and with a rending crash of metal I left the end of the catapult with the cradle still firmly attached to my Seafire, which, understandably, was descending fast under all that extra weight. By extraordinary luck, the cradle and my Seafire parted company at the *moment critique*!

The Seafire Mk III had by now entered service, although the only unit operating this more extensively navalised Merlin-engined model outside the United Kingdom was 889 Squadron, which was serving on board the escort carrier HMS *Atheling* in the Indian Ocean and which, at this time, was endeavouring to distract Japanese attention from the American landings in the Marianas in concert with *Illustrious*, the fighter element aboard which comprised Corsairs. It was on this side of the world that the Seafire was to see most action, although it was to fail to eradicate the unfavourable impression that it had created during 'Avalanche' and attrition resulting from landing accidents remained high, despite the growing experience of its pilots. Indeed, those that had doubted the wisdom of adapting the Spitfire for shipboard operations from the outset saw more than fulfilled many of their misgivings concerning the structural integrity of this fighter operating in a scenario for which it had not been designed.

MORE ROAR

Captain Eric Brown CBE DSC AFC

THE potential of the Griffon-engined Spitfire had meanwhile impressed Their Lordships of the Admiralty sufficiently for them to have expressed keen interest in a similarly powered Seafire, and on 21 February 1943 Jeffrey Quill had dropped in to Arbroath in a Griffon-engined Spitfire Mk XII, staying for a couple of days of deck-landing instruction on our dummy deck which had been laid out with arrester wires on a short runway. I had been moved on to this more powerful Spitfire at once, and if I had thought flying the Seafire L. Mk IIC to be an exhilarating experience it had been as nothing compared with this: the throaty growl of the Griffon III engine, the superlative low-level speed and the very fine roll rate, owing much to its clipped wings, combined to produce sheer magic. I had taken this beauty aboard HMS *Indomitable* on 9 March, and had completed the routine series of fifteen deck landings with no trouble at all.

One year and five weeks later, in the afternoon of 26 March 1944, I landed the first prototype (NS487) of the Griffon-engined Seafire aboard HMS *Indefatigable* for the first time; I had landed-on a Mosquito during the course of the morning of the same day, such being the panic of that period of the war. This, the Seafire Mk XV, which had been evolved to Specification N. 4/43 (and the mark number of which reflected an attempt on the part of officialdom to introduce some logic into the designating of members of the closely related Spitfire and Seafire lines of development, its immediate predecessor having been the Spitfire Mk XIV), was something of a mongrel if such may be said of any member of so thoroughbred a family.

The Seafire Mk XV utilised the L. Mk III airframe to which had been added the wing-root fuel tanks of the Spitfire Mk IX and the retractable tailwheel and enlarged vertical surfaces of the Spitfire Mk VIII. This amalgam had been mated with a naval version of the Griffon engine, the Mk VI, offering combat ratings of 1,815hp at 4,500 feet and 1,730hp at 13,000 feet at 2,740rpm and with plus 15 pounds boost. The fuel tankage had been rearranged to produce a slight gain in internal capacity at 100 Imperial gallons, and the heavier (and rather thirstier) engine permitted the provision of a weightier, more highly stressed hook, though still of the A-frame type. Although the nose was lengthened as a result of the longer engine and substantial fairings on the upper part of the cowling enclosed enlarged rocker boxes, the view forward was not noticeably inferior to that of the Merlin-engined models owing to the Griffon's lower thrust line.

The Griffon engine was, of course, 'left-handed' as opposed to the Merlin, and the incidence of the wing of this model had to be reversed to help balance out the torque effect—a change which in itself was to present a quota of new problems—and the enlarged rudder alleviating the yaw. But a new problem arose on take-off. At take-off boost of 15 pounds, the aircraft could be kept straight by the use of full rudder trim and rudder pedal application, but it tracked bodily to starboard in a series of hops, these carrying it towards the island superstructure. For this reason, and because the take-off distance was good, I recommended that take-off power be limited normally to plus 10 pounds boost. This tracking characteristic was so marked that on tarmac runways the inner canvas lining of the starboard tyre was exposed after an average of five take-offs at plus 15 pounds boost, and, despite the reversal of wing incidence, there was still a considerable torque roll effect which dipped the starboard wing during the take-off run.

The results of these trials were discussed at a meeting at the Ministry of Aircraft Production on 6 April 1944, with relevance to the possible conversion of the Spitfire Mk XXI for naval use, and it was agreed that a contra-rotating propeller should be introduced at the earliest opportunity to eliminate the tracking, while throttle travel should be increased to afford coarser engine control.

A further stage in the refinement of the Seafire Mk XV was reached a month later, on 12 May, when I made the first tail-down catapult launch with the first prototype. The tail-down launching system meant that we could do away with the ugly and weighty catapult spools, which protruded from the

Below: First of the Griffons: NS487, the first prototype Seafire Mk XV. Early production aircraft retained the A-frame arrester hook seen here. Again, the use of orthochromatic film has distorted the true tonal values.

flanks of the aircraft like knobs from the neck of Frankenstein's monster, and replace them with a single hook under the centre section and a holdback point at the tail. It offered the added advantage that the aircraft took off in the optimum three-point attitude as opposed to an attitude parallel to that of the line of flight.

Above: A Westland-built Seafire XV finished, for reasons unknown, in an immaculate glossy black and Sky colour scheme, with an 'aluminium' spinner. Aft of the engine firewall, the Mk XV's fuselage was little different from that of the Mk III. This example, however, has the later 'sting' type arrester hook which was standard on all subsequent Seafires
Below: The author demonstrates his prowess as Mk XV NS487 takes the wire perfectly during carrier-compatibility trials, August 1945. Notice that the aircraft in fact has both types of arrester hook fitted; the 'sting' type hook is being utilised for this particular landing.

While the strengthened A-frame hook was to be retained for the first few hundred production Seafire Mk XVs in the event, the second prototype (NS490), which arrived at the RAE Farnborough during July, was fitted with a new hook of the 'sting' type which lay horizontally beneath the base of the rudder and moved aft when lowered before adopting the trailing position. The hook was now fitted in the optimum position, permitting a marked increase in the range of aircraft attitude when deck landing, and shortly after the arrival of NS490 at Farnborough, I took NS487—by now also fitted with a 'sting' type hook—on board HMS *Implacable*. On 28 August I performed a series of fifteen deck landings, the aircraft by this time having been fitted with a new throttle control box which had the quadrant increased by 80 per cent so that the greater travel reduced the sensitivity of power increase with throttle movement. The throttle was also gated 'Take-Off' (plus 10 pounds boost) and 'Combat' (plus fifteen pounds) as recommended at the MAP meeting in the previous April.

With its increased (11 per cent) horn balance on the elevators, which improved speed control on the approach, and the markedly enhanced safety factor of the 'sting' hook, we were getting much nearer in our quest for a Seafire with reasonably good deck landing characteristics. I felt that the hook could be lengthened further with benefit, but the Seafire was, like its land-based stablemate, a very clean aircraft and lack of drag allowed it to float over the arrester wires if its approach speed was imprecise. I suggested, therefore, that, in addition to lengthening the hook, a five-bladed propeller be adopted to produce more braking effect on cutting the throttle. Of course, the Seafire would never have been remotely acceptable for deck landing but for its innocuous stalling characteristics. For example, the Seafire Mk XV all-down stall occurred at 57 knots, with only a gentle drop of the nose preceded by mild buffeting and a slight twitch on the ailerons.

In mid-October I was aboard *Pretoria Castle* with two of the Seafire Mk XV prototypes, one with a lengthened 'sting' hook and the other with the earlier A-frame hook but with an extra fine pitch propeller to assist braking in the landing configuration by presenting more of a 'disc'. The longer hook was a great success and the finer-pitch propeller partially successful. A month later, I took three Seafire Mk XVs aboard *Pretoria Castle*, each embodying some modifications previously advocated. The second prototype (NS490) had the 'sting' hook and fined-off propeller (the fine pitch stop being advanced two degrees), the fourth prototype (PK240) retained the A-frame hook but had been fitted with a five-bladed propeller, and a production example (SR448)—actually the third off the Westland line—mated A-frame hook and fined-off propeller with controllable radiator flaps and stronger wheels and tyres. These trials really finalised the 'sting' hook as standard for all future Seafires, together with the increased throttle quadrant as fitted to all the trials aircraft and the two-degree fine pitch stop, the five-bladed propeller eventually being adopted for the somewhat abortive Seafire Mk 45.

While the production tempo of the Seafire Mk XV was building up, the fighter had been going through yet further stages in its evolution which was, of course, now firmly wedded to the Griffon engine—although no Seafires with this powerplant were destined to see service in World War II.

Westland had been busily refining the basic Mk XV, the company's attention being directed primarily towards further improvements to the undercarriage, enhanced all-round pilot vision and increased internal fuel capacity. The third prototype Mk XV (NS493) had been used by Westland to test various modifications, the most obvious being the cutting down of the aft fuselage decking to the level of the upper longerons and the application of a frameless 'bubble' canopy, and this change was to be applied to the final thirty Mk XVs off the assembly line and to be standardised for the next variant, the Seafire Mk XVII.

The Seafire Mk XVII was more noteworthy, however, for the markedly superior undercarriage that it was eventually to introduce. In November

Opposite page, top: SX277, a Seafire Mk XVII. This mark introduced the clear, 'teardrop' sliding canopy to the *genre* (although some Mk XVs were so fitted) and also featured strengthened wings, greater fuel capacity, a 24-volt (replacing the earlier 12-volt) electrical system and, in later production aircraft, a more resilient undercarriage.
Left: A Seafire Mk XV in service with 1832 Squadron RNVR at Stretton. The open flap on the wing-root fairing offers access to the electrical system.
This page, top: SX334 was the prototype Mk XVII. The additional fuel tank sited behind the pilot has in this aircraft been removed to facilitate the carriage of two F.24 cameras, the ports for which are clearly evident.
Above: The same aircraft seen from aft. A further innovation for the Griffon-engined Seafires was the provision of a retractable tailwheel.

1945, before the application of the new undercarriage, I took the Mk XVII through its RATOG proofing tests. Like the Mk XV, this aircraft tracked bodily to starboard, and I suspected that this characteristic would become heavily accentuated when asymmetric firing was attempted with the starboard rocket failed; indeed, I was convinced that in such circumstances a collision with the carrier's island structure would be inevitable. In the following March, I was to have the opportunity to confirm my conviction concerning the behaviour of the Seafire Mk XVII, and, for that matter, the Mk XV, under conditions of asymmetric RATOG firing and, as a result, these 'first generation' Griffon-engined Seafires were never to use RATOG at sea unless ranged forward of the first crash barrier position on the carrier flight deck.

Subsequently, in January 1946, the first Seafire Mk XVII fitted with the long-stroke undercarriage was to come to the RAE for checking out before the application of this new gear on the production line.

CONTRA-PROP

Captain Eric Brown CBE DSC AFC

SPECIFICATION N.7/44 had earlier been formulated for a Seafire equivalent to the Spitfire Mk 21, which mated wings that were entirely new in both plan and profile with the new two-stage Griffon. Assigned the designation Seafire Mk 45, a prototype (TM379) was produced by the adaptation of a standard Spitfire Mk 21, the only concession to its nautical rôle consisting of modified mainwheel fairing plates to increase arrester wire clearance, the installation of naval R/T and the application of 'sting' type hook and slinging points. In mid-November 1944 TM379 had come to Farnborough for arresting proofing. This had gone splendidly, and on the 23rd of that month I had taken the Griffon 61-powered aeroplane aboard *Pretoria Castle* for its initial deck trials, landing on at 9,250 pounds, some 1,200 pounds more than the clean loaded weight of the Seafire Mk XVII.

I found the Seafire Mk 45 prototype easier to deck land than, say, the Mk XV, but the view forward had deteriorated slightly and aileron control was less effective. The approach speed was 75 knots and the stalling characteristics had certainly worsened, there being virtually no warning before a wing dropped and the all-down stall occurring at 58 knots. The performance increase with the two-stage Griffon was, of course, significant—one of the fifty production examples later built (LA494) was to attain the equivalent of Mach = 0.88 in a dive at 35,000 feet a year or so later—and a very high roll rate was possible, but this improved performance had been achieved at some cost to handling. Substantial trim changes were demanded with variations of power and the very much greater output of the two-stage engine combined with the five-bladed propeller to produce an unpleasant swinging tendency during take-off. In fact, the throttle had to be advanced somewhat gingerly, and then no more than plus seven pounds of boost could be used, and even with full left rudder a predilection for swinging to starboard and crabbing remained.

Whereas the Seafire Mk XVII had been considered somewhat as an interim model pending introduction of the two-stage Griffon, so the Mk 45 was viewed as a development aircraft rather than as a potential embarked operational fighter pending availability of the six-bladed contra-prop intended for application to the ultimate Seafire development. Thus only fifty Seafire Mk 45s were built, these being produced at Castle Bromwich during the latter part of 1945 and subsequently giving the maintenance people innumerable headaches owing to their inordinate demands on servicing time.

The contra-prop had duly appeared on TM379, which had returned to the RAE as the prototype Seafire Mk 46 in June 1945, but the Mk 46 was destined to be yet another interim model as the folding arrangement for the new wing introduced with the Mk 45 had still to be finalised. Thus, like its immediate predecessor, the Mk 46 embodied minimum 'navalisation', although it did incorporate more of the features that were to be standardised on the definitive Seafire Mk 47 which was to bring the production career of the sea-legged Spitfire to a close. For example, the frameless 'bubble' canopy reappeared, together with the wing 'wet' points permitting 'combat tanks' to be carried, and RATOG points were provided. Of course, the most important innovation was the Griffon 87 engine driving two three-bladed contra-rotating propellers, which quite transformed the characteristics of the

Below: LA443, a Seafire Mk 45. This mark was regarded as an interim development and, in the event, proved disappointing in a number of respects.

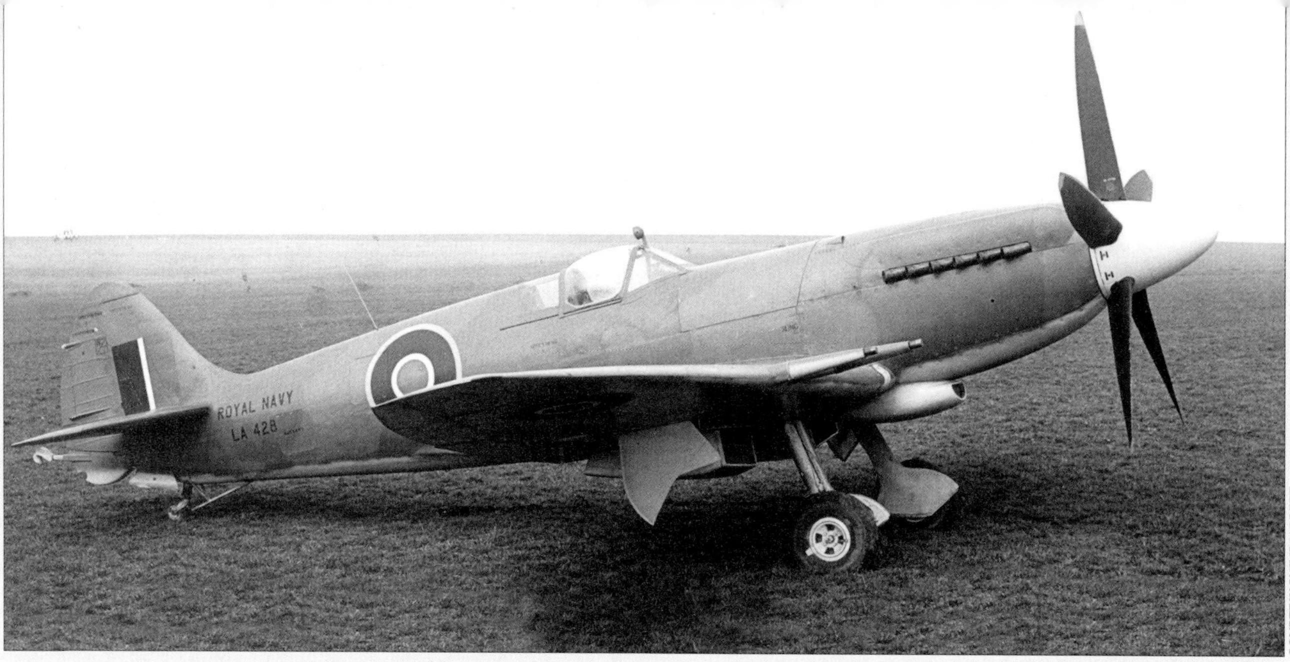

COURTESY PHILIP JARRETT

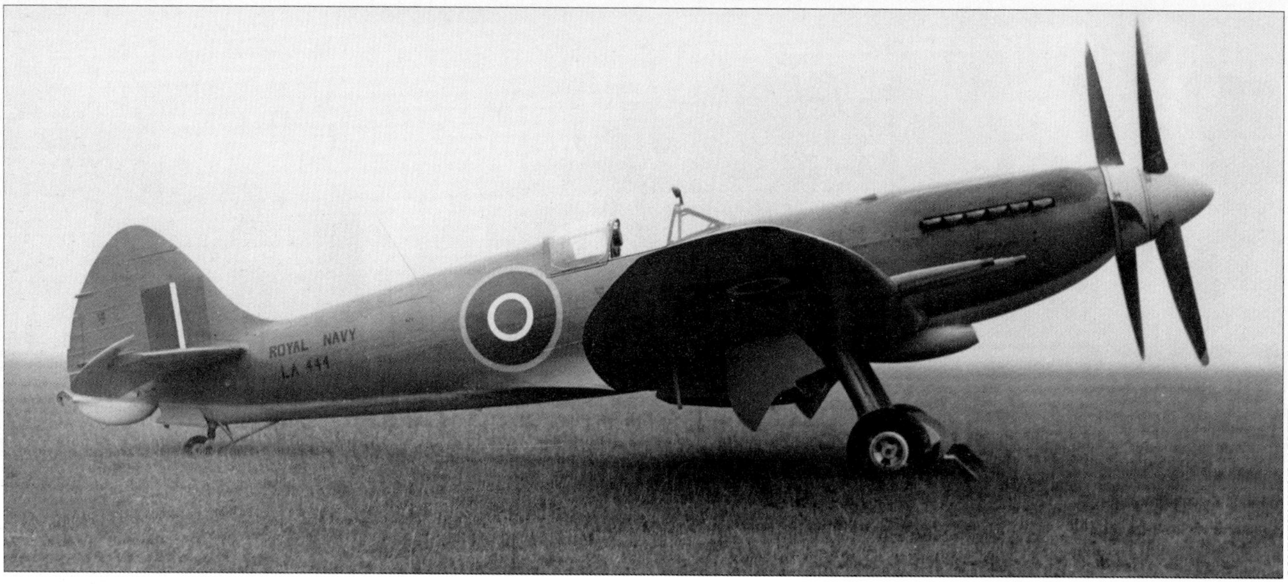

COURTESY PHILIP JARRETT

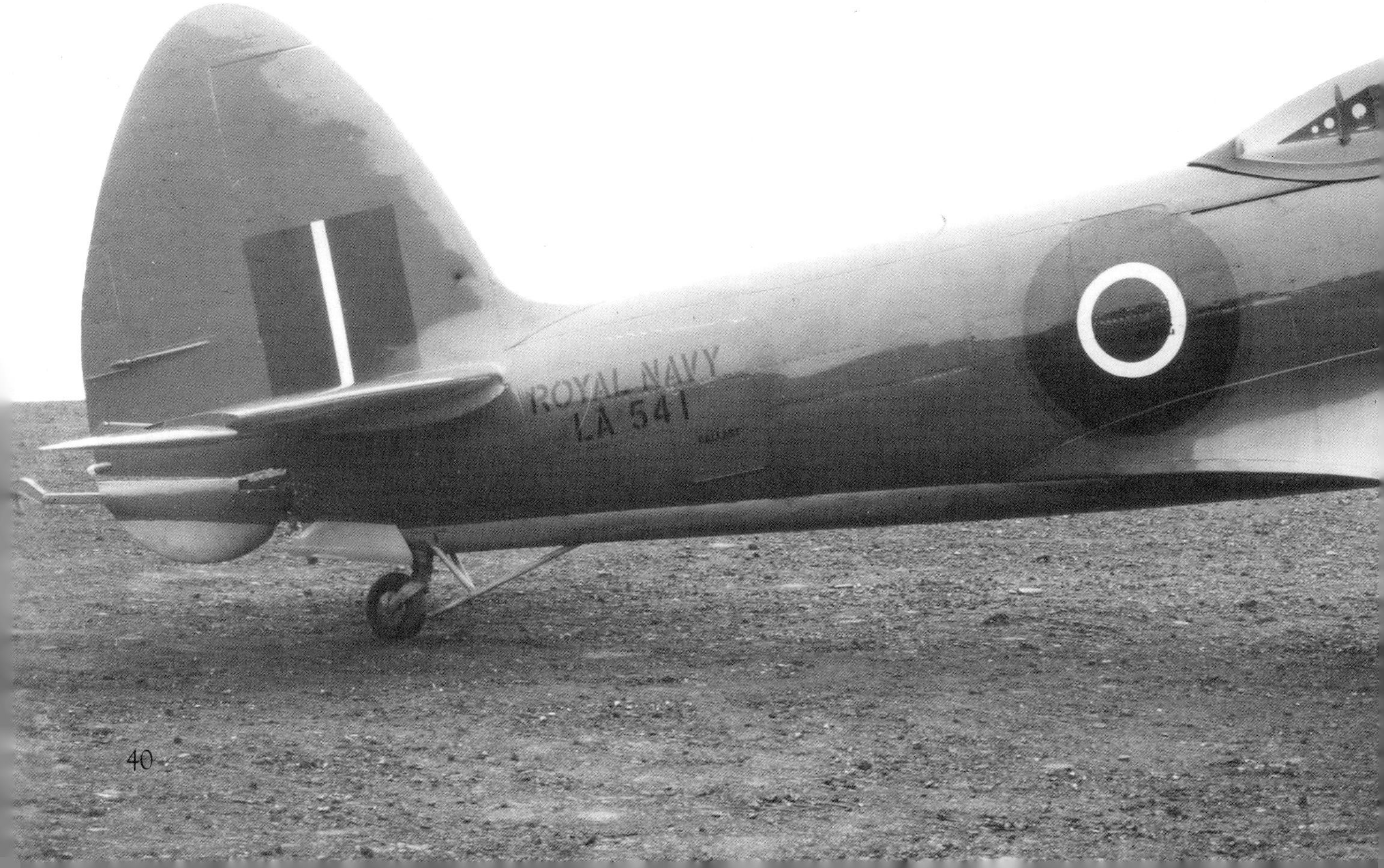

fighter, eliminating most of the more 'uncomfortable' aspects of the Mk 45.

After completing arresting proofing with the prototype Mk 46, I took it aboard *Pretoria Castle* on 12 July 1945, making ten landings down to a wind speed of 16 knots. From the outset I became aware that this was by far the easiest Seafire of them all to operate from a deck. Full power up to plus 18 pounds boost could be applied for take-off with rudder neutral and the aircraft ran straight as a die, the run itself being so short as to render catapulting superfluous. It was indeed a delightful machine: variations of power were no longer demanding on trim—loops and rolls could be effected without any call for rudder corrections if the aircraft was properly trimmed—and the contra-prop gave very powerful braking on cutting the throttle. In fact, so strong was this braking effect that the stick had to be pulled back as the throttle was cut because the nose otherwise pitched down sharply.

The war now being over, little sense of urgency was attached to getting the fully navalised, two-stage Griffon-powered Seafire Mk 47 into carrier service and, indeed, the first production example was not destined to appear until early 1947, but between April 1946 and October of the following year a succession of all marks of Griffon-engined Seafire nevertheless passed through my hands on RATOG, arresting and catapult trials at overload weights festooned with a bewildering variety of external stores. There were occasional problems when hardware broke loose, but after a short spell of 'back to the drawing board', these were invariably resolved. Overload weights attained during these trials included 9,775 pounds with the Seafire Mk XVII and 12,490 pounds with the Mk 47. When one considers that the normal loaded weight of the Seafire Mk IB had been 6,718 pounds, some measure may be gauged of the dramatic development of this fighter that had taken place over a few short years.

It has been said of the Spitfire 20 series and their sea-legged offspring that they were no longer *true* 'fires, but this I cannot really accept. It is true that

Left, upper: The Mk 45 was a direct development of the RAF's Spitfire Mk 21 and did not, therefore, feature the 'teardrop' canopy of the Mk XVII. LA428 is depicted here.
Left, lower: Mk 45 LA444 was fitted with a Griffon 85 driving contra-rotating propellers. The definitive 'naval Spitfire' was now close to hand.
Below: The first production Seafire Mk 46, LA541, clearly showing the type's 'teardrop' canopy and enlarged vertical tail surfaces.

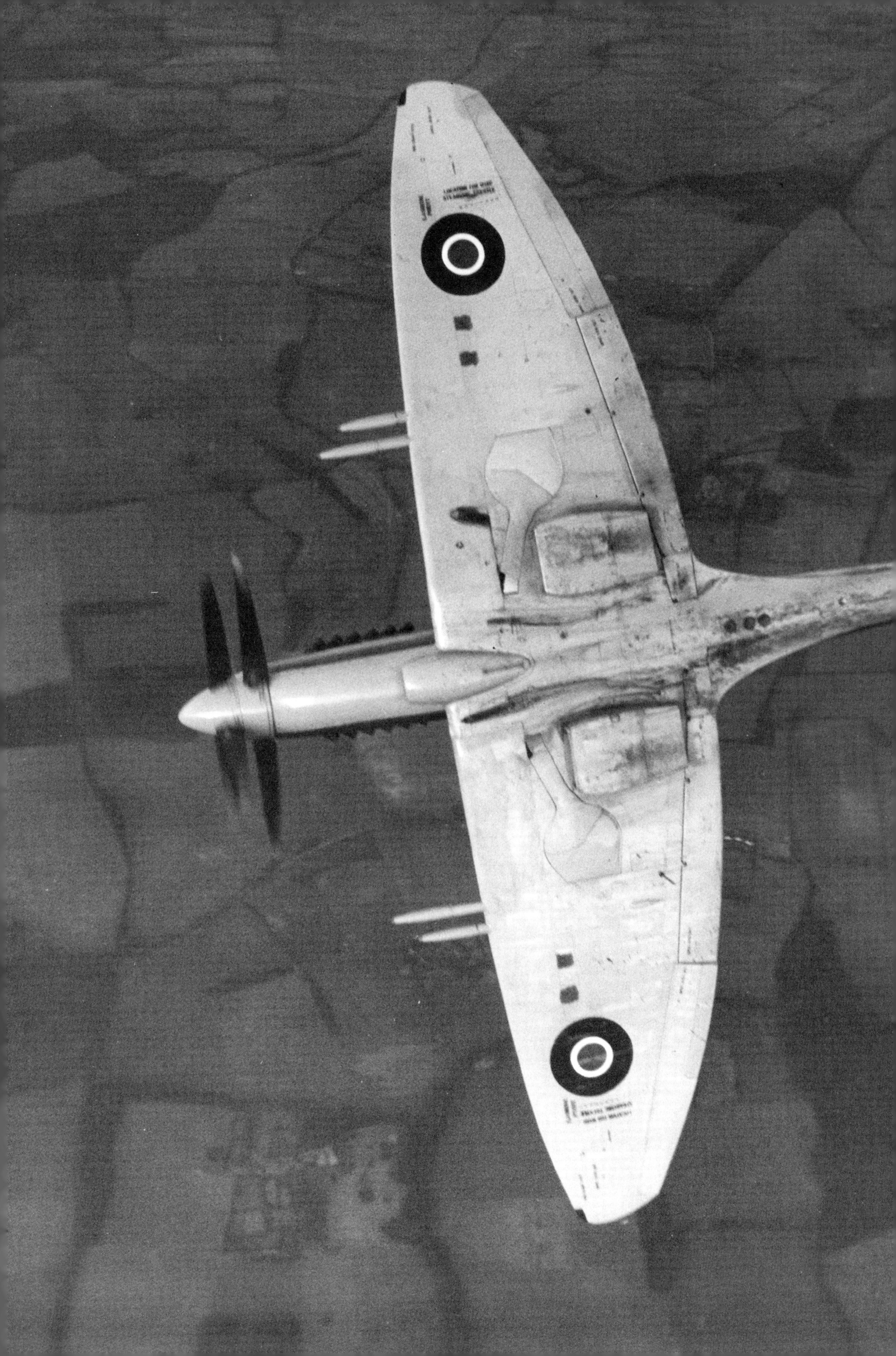

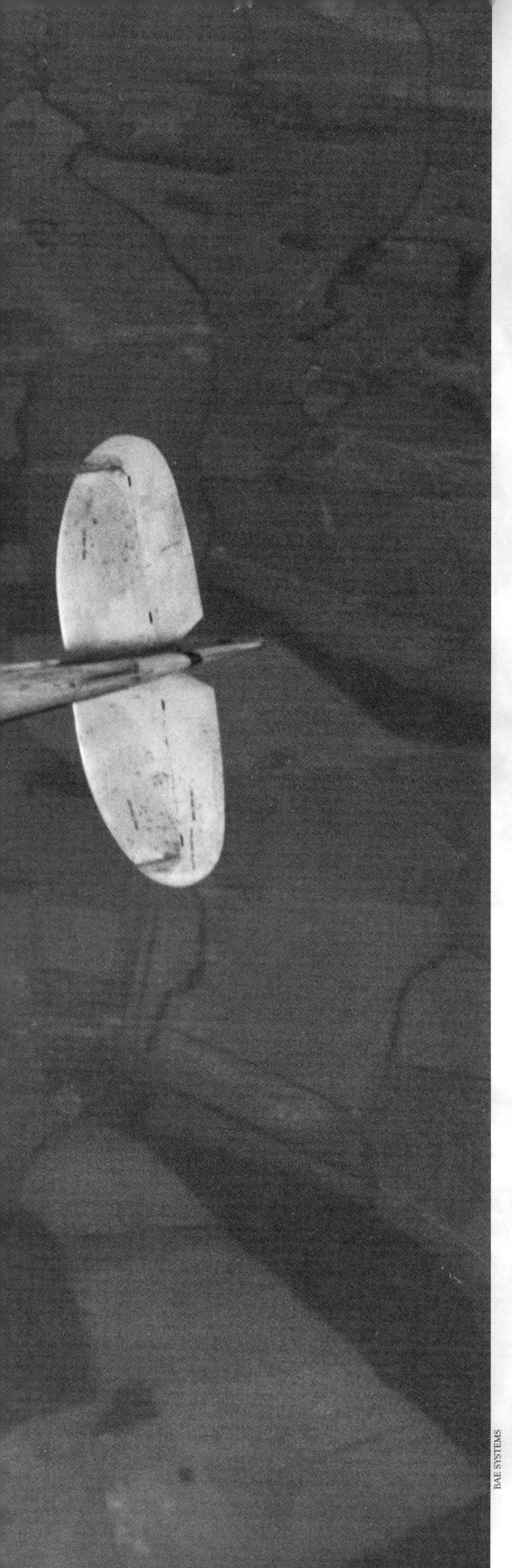

very few details remained unaltered during their production lives, but the design principles and basic configuration on which they were originally founded persisted throughout. Really fundamental changes were proposed from time to time, but the advantages that such offered were too nebulous to render worthwhile any radical departure from the tried and proven, and the final production versions of both Spitfire and Seafire, end products of a continuous process of incremental design development though they undoubtedly were, remained, in my view at least, essentially refinements of Reginald Mitchell's original design. Despite the innumerable changes, surprisingly little aesthetic beauty of line had been lost—although, admittedly, the tail suffered somewhat—and none of the beautiful harmony of control.

The Seafire Mk 47 differed little externally from its immediate predecessor, but featured hydraulically operated wing folding (although the first dozen or so off the line had manual folding), the actual fold consisting of a single break immediately outboard of the cannon bay and the outboard panel folding upwards through 90 degrees. A Griffon 88 was standardised, this differing from the Griffon 87 in having a Rolls-Royce-developed injection system in place of the original Bendix-Stromberg fuel-metering carburettor. Large-area flaps were provided, their deflection being reduced by ten degrees to improve arrester wire clearance, and immense vertical tail surfaces similar to those evolved for the Spiteful made their appearance.

An impressive length of nose stretched ahead of the pilot seated in the cockpit of the Seafire Mk 47, but, unlike that of, say, the Firebrand, it did not seem obtrusive. Despite the growth in sophistication of the Seafire's equipment with the passage of the years, the layout of the instrumentation remained neat, although the cockpit was perhaps austere by American shipboard fighter standards of the day. No provision was made for cockpit heating, for example, and there was certainly not overmuch space for a pilot of even my relatively compact stature, while a pilot of more than average height surely experienced discomfort during protracted sorties.

The Griffon 88 was started on the lower main (48 Imperial gallon) fuel tank. Incidentally, as a result of the progressive increases in total fuel capacity—with overload fuel the Mk 47 had an endurance of four hours and a range in excess of 800nm—and the

Left: Seafire LA542, the second production Mk 46, is put through its paces. No front-line FAA squadrons received this particular version of the aircraft.

Above: The ultimate piston-engined naval fighter—the Seafire Mk 47. VP447 is seen here awaiting its first flight, February 1948.
Below: PS948 conducting deck-landing trials on board HMS *Illustrious*, May 1947; notice the safety barrier rigged at far left. This aircraft was one of the first pre-production batch of Mk 47s.

Opposite, top: Mk 47 VP474, allocated to 1833 Squadron RNVR based at Bramcote, performs a take-off assisted by RATOG. The fittings for the latter are little changed in design from those produced for the early Seafires.

number of tanks involved (which could total as many as ten), fuel management procedures had become rather more complex than was the case with preceding Seafire models. The cock just below the centre of the instrument panel was turned to 'On', the fuel booster pump was switched to 'Main' and activated for 10–15 seconds, a single stroke was made of the priming pump, the ignition was switched 'On', the Coffman starter cartridge was fired (the starter push-button being kept depressed to operate the booster coil), and the Griffon usually burst into life with a delightful throaty roar.

During the warm-up at 1,200–1,400rpm after oil pressure had steadied, the normal checks of constant-speed propeller, two-speed supercharger, generator, magnetos and brake pressure were carried out. Taxying was effortless, as with all Seafires, but the Mk 47 was very nose heavy and care had to be exercised when applying the brakes in consequence. From a carrier deck the take-off was made with the elevator trimmed one division nose-up, the radiator shutters switched 'Open' and the flaps at 'Take-off'. The surge of acceleration at plus 18 pounds boost and 2,750rpm was electrifying, and the climb at this power to 1,000 feet was so rapid that the pilot was hard pushed to retract the undercarriage and flaps before passing this altitude, at which power had to be reduced to plus nine pounds and 2,600rpm.

Below: Mk 47 PS946 reveals its undersurfaces during a test flight. Right: The Mk 47 was the only Seafire to incorporate powered wing-folding—an innovation that saved both time and manpower during the flight-deck cycle.

The maximum climb speed was 150 knots, with the supercharger changing automatically into high gear at around 10,000 feet so that this speed was maintained up to 25,000 feet, which was reached in a little over nine minutes. Thereafter, speed was reduced by three knots per thousand feet, but the Seafire was still climbing at something of the order of 3,000 feet a minute, passing 30,000 feet in about 10.5 minutes. This definitive Seafire model certainly excelled in climbing, and few other production piston-engined fighters could match it let alone surpass it.

The supreme feature of the Mk 47, as with all Seafires, was its superlative control harmony, which, combined with its performance, rendered it an outstanding combat fighter. Control response and manœuvrability could hardly be faulted, and a 360-degree turn entered at 270 knots IAS at 10,000 feet was effected within 25 seconds. All normal aerobatics could be performed with ease, although inverted flight had to be restricted owing to the rapid fall in oil pressure, and the recommended IAS for a loop was 300–320 knots, with 180–220 knots for a roll, 320–340 knots for a roll off a loop and 350–400 knots for an upward roll. True, the rate of roll was marginally lower than that achieved by earlier Seafires, and particularly those with clipped wings, but it was impressive nonetheless and superior to that of most contemporaries.

Acceleration was good and from 200 knots at 10,000 feet it would reach 270 knots at full power within a minute, while in level flight at 20,500 feet a speed of 392 knots was attainable. Although longitudinally and directionally stable, it was somewhat unstable laterally owing to friction in the aileron control circuit. It was very fast indeed in a dive, and with the Rolls-Royce injector pump that had supplanted the Bendix-Stromberg carburettor of earlier versions of the two-stage Griffon it could be bunted straight into a vertical dive without a trace of engine falter, but the immense rudder and the rudder trim tab had to be handled with some care as sudden application produced violent skidding.

The mild stalling characteristics, although not perhaps as completely innocuous on the Mk 47 as on early Seafires, made it an aircraft that could be flown to the limits of manœuvrability with complete impunity, but vision, which had been reduced laterally as a result of the introduction of curved sidescreens, left a lot to be desired in inclement weather, and the lack of windscreen wiper aggravated the condition which was still further impaired at low speeds by the tail-down attitude adopted by the aircraft. Nevertheless, it was still the easiest of all Seafires to deck land, although, anomalously enough, it was probably the most difficult to land ashore.

Circuit speed was 170 knots, at which the hood could be opened, the booster pump switched on for the tank in use and the radiator shutters opened. The undercarriage was lowered at about 150 knots and the selector lever returned to 'Idle'. The propeller rpm were set to 2,600 and the flaps were lowered. The turn on to the final approach on an airfield was made at 120 knots and the propeller rpm control lever set fully forward while speed was gradually reduced to 90 knots. The aircraft normally wheeled on to the runway to give improved view and avoid the possibility of a bounce as the throttle was cut, for the nose of the Seafire Mk 47 then tended to drop unless positively corrected.

Below: Another view of PS948 on board HMS *Illustrious*. Contra-rotating propellers eliminated the tendency for an aircraft to drift during take-off and landing as a result of the 'torque effect' induced by a single propeller.

SPECIFICATIONS

SUPERMARINE SEAFIRE Mks IB, IIC, III, XV, XVII, 45, 46 and 47 and SEAFANG

Mk	IB	IIC	L.IIC	III	L.III
Powerplant:	One R-R Merlin 45/46 = 1,515hp	One R-R Merlin 45/46 = 1,515hp	One R-R Merlin 32 = 1,645hp	One R-R Merlin 55 = 1,600hp	One R-R Merlin 55M = 1,585hp
Dimensions					
Length (oa)	30ft 2½in (9.21m)	30ft 2½in (9.21m)	30ft 2½in (9.21m)	30ft 2½in (9.21m)	30ft 2½in (9.21m)
Wing span	36ft 10in (11.23m)	36ft 10in (11.23m)	32ft 7in (9.93m)	36ft 10in (11.23m)	32ft 7in (9.93m)
(folded)	—	—	—	14ft 3in (4.34m)	14ft 3in (4.34m)
Height (oa)	11ft 2½in (3.42m)	11ft 2½in (3.42m)	11ft 2½in (3.42m)	11ft 5½in (3.49m)	11ft 5½in (3.49m)
Wing area	242.0 sq ft (22.48m^2)	242.0 sq ft (22.48m^2)	234.0 sq ft (21.74m^2)	242.0 sq ft (22.48m^2)	234.0 sq ft (21.74m^2)
Weights:					
Empty	5,910lb (2,680kg)	6,100lb (2,765kg)	6,110lb (2,770kg)	6,200lb (2,810kg)	6,200lb (2,810kg)
Loaded	6,700lb (3,040kg)	7,000lb (3,175kg)	7,000lb (3,175kg)	7,200lb (3,265kg)	7,200lb (3,265kg)
Armament:	2 × 20mm cannon, 4 × 0.303in MG	2 × 20mm cannon, 4 × 0.303in MG	2 × 20mm cannon, 4 × 0.303in MG	2 × 20mm cannon, 4 × 0.303in MG	2 × 20mm cannon, 4 × 0.303in MG
Performance:					
Max. speed	308kts (355mph, 572kph) at 13,000ft (3,960m)	300kts (345mph, 555kph) at 19,000ft (5,790m)	304kts (350mph, 564kph) at 15,000ft (4,570m)	304kts (350mph, 564kph) at 15,000t (4,570m)	313kts (360mph, 580kph) at 5,000ft (1,525m)
Climb (initial)	2,950ft/min (900m/min)	2,950ft/min (900m/min)	2,950ft/min (900m/min)	3,250ft/min (990m/min)	4,160ft/min (1,260m/min)
Service ceiling	31,000ft (9,450m)	31,000ft (9,450m)	31,000ft (9,450m)	32,000ft (9,750m)	30,000ft (9,150m)
Range (normal)	434nm (500 miles, 800km)	434nm (500 miles, 800km)	434nm (500 miles, 800km)	443nm (510 miles, 820km)	443nm (510 miles, 820km)
Number built	166	Total Mk II production 372		Total Mk III production 1,250	

Manufacturer: The Supermarine Aviation Works (Vickers) Ltd, Woolston, Southampton. Chief Designer: Joseph Smith.

XV	XVII	45	46	47	Seafang
1 × R-R Griffon VI = 1,850hp	1 × R-R Griffon VI = 1,850hp	1 × R-R Griffon 61 = 2,030hp	1 × R-R Griffon 85 = 2,375hp	1 × R-R Griffon 88 = 2,350hp	1 × R-R Griffon 89 = 2,350hp
32ft 3in (9.83m)	32ft 3in (9.83m)	33ft 7in (10.24m)	33ft 7in (10.24m)	34ft 4in (10.46m)	34ft 1in (10.39m)
36ft 10in (11.23m)	36ft 10in (11.23m)	36ft 11in (11.25m)	36ft 11in (11.25m)	36ft 11in (11.25m)	35ft 0in (10.67m)
14ft 1in (4.65m)	14ft 1in (4.65m)	—	—	18ft 11in (5.77m)	
10ft 8½in (3.26m)	10ft 8½in (3.26m)	12ft 6½in (3.82m)	12ft 6½in (3.82m)	12ft 6½in (3.82m)	12ft 6½in (3.82m)
242.0 sq ft (22.49m^2)	242.0 sq ft (22.49m^2)	244.0 sq ft (22.68m^2)	244.0 sq ft (22.68m^2)	243.6 sq ft (22.63m^2)	210.0 sq ft (19.52m^2)
6,300lb (2,855kg)	6,385lb (2,895kg)	Unavailable	7,100lb (3,220kg)	7,625lb (3,460kg)	8,000lb (3,630kg)
8,000lb (3,630kg)	8,150lb (3,695kg)	Unavailable	9,400lb (4,265kg)	10,200lb (4,625kg)	10,450lb (4,740kg)
2 × 20mm cannon, 4 × 0.303in MG	2 × 20mm cannon, 4 × 0.303in MG	4 × 20mm cannon	4 × 20mm cannon	4 × 20mm cannon	4 × 20mm cannon
335kts (385mph, 620kph) at 15,000ft (4,570m)	340kts (392mph, 630kph) at 15,000ft (4,570m)	Unavailable	385kts (443mph, 715kph) at 25,000ft (7,620m)	393kts (452mph, 730kph) at 20,000ft (7,000m)	413kts (475mph, 765kph) at 21,000ft (6,400m)
4,500ft/min (1,370m/min)	4,500ft/min (1,370m/min)	Unavailable	3,750ft/min (1,145m/min)	4,790ft/min (1,460m/min)	4,630ft/min (1,410m/min)
35,500ft (10,820m)	35,500ft (10,820m)	Unavailable	41,000ft (12,450m)	43,100ft (13,140m)	41,000ft (12,450m)
375nm (430 miles, 692km)	375nm (435 miles, 700km)	Unavailable	375nm (435 miles, 700km)	350nm (405 miles, 650km)	340nm (390 miles, 630km)
390	234	51	26	90	9

Above: SX336, alias G-KASX, is the only airworthy Seafire based in Britain, and, at the time of writing, one of only three in the world. It was restored by Kennet Aviation at North Weald and flew once more on 3 May 2006.

MORE FROM THE COCKPIT

Exaggerating the Drop *Commander Geoffrey Higgs* AFC

Having successfully completed my pilot training in Canada, I was recommended for flying fighters and thus avoided the inevitable Barracuda, which was the unenviable lot of those selected for TBR training. In due course I arrived at No 1 Naval Air Fighter School, Yeovilton, where the course was split in two groups: those assigned to the Vought Corsair IV would remain at Yeovilton whilst the remainder would go to Henstridge, a satellite airfield fifteen miles to the east, for Seafire training. I was selected for Corsair training.

It was a fortuitous choice, since it gave me the opportunity to fly the Corsair and the Hellcat in front-line squadrons, which would have been denied to me had I been sent to Henstridge for the Seafire OTU, since, when World War II came to an end, the terms of Lend-Lease required the return or disposal of all American-built aircraft. At the time I had mixed feelings. I think my heart was set on flying the Seafire, but the reputation of the Corsair had gone before it; however, by the time I made the Seafire's acquaintance I was sold on the Corsair and it never let me down. The second part of my good fortune was that, not long after the conclusion of the war, I was appointed to a front-line Seafire squadron shortly to be embarked in HMS *Theseus*. I thus had the best of both worlds.

My initial impressions of the Seafire were firstly, how small it was compared with the American aircraft I had flown, and secondly, that it was something of an enigma. In the air it became a part of you, like no other aircraft; it was easy and a joy to fly, with seemingly few vices other than distinctly heavy ailerons and a reluctance to turn at near its maximum speed—which would, obviously, be a handicap in air-to-air combat. On the ground or in the course of carrier operations, however, things were rather different. Its narrow undercarriage made landing in gusty or cross-wind conditions tricky, whilst taxying over rough ground required care, particularly with the aircraft's nose-heavy tendency to lurch forward.

In short, the Seafire was at home in the air but not on the ground. As a deck-landing aircraft it possessed the most undesirable qualities imaginable. Apart from the ridiculously narrow undercarriage, which took no prisoners if the pilot landed with 'drift on', the aircraft was uncomfortable in the inevitable turbulence short of the round-down, especially when the margin for a successful landing from the approach speed of around 68 knots was plus or minus two knots. Even near the stall, in the high winds encountered over the flight deck, the Seafire tended to float when about to touch down, owing to the absence of drag in this beautifully clean aircraft. If the view over the nose during a carrier approach, which was hardly exciting, is taken into consideration, it all added up to makeshift carrier aeroplane—which of course is what it was.

Left: A nasty 'prang' by a Seafire III, halted by the barrier after, it would seem, bouncing over the wires. The forward fuselage has sheared at the engine firewall and the pilot is beginning to scramble out of the cockpit.
Opposite: With plenty of 'goofers' in attendance, an RNVR Seafire Mk 17 pilot (1831 Squadron) skims the barrier after attempting a landing on board HMS *Illustrious* during DLT. As can be seen from the positions of the ailerons, strenuous efforts are being made in the cockpit to level the aircraft: the pilot has moved the stick to the right to correct his considerable plight but at his reduced speed his chances are not good.

During the deployment of HMS *Theseus* to the Far East and Australasia on a goodwill tour after the war, the Seafire squadrons of both *Theseus* (804 NAS) and HMS *Glory* (806 NAS), which joined us at Singapore, sustained the dismal record of the aircraft for carrier landings. In the case of *Theseus*'s air group, much of this was due to inadequate attention paid by the Naval Staffs to the need for reasonable continuity in planning flying schedules, particularly later on during the Australia section of the tour when the high pressure of 'showing the flag' entertainment took precedence over safe flying practice.

In a deployment of ten months, Seafire deck-landing accidents ranged from an aircraft stalling on the approach with fatal consequences, to undercarriage failure arising from landing with a small amount of drift on, a landing well to port causing a collision with the batsman's platform screen, numerous 'but for the grace of God' incidents and the inevitable barrier entries of which this writer contributed two! On reflection, it is likely that in both cases—in the second of which I caught the last wire but nudged the barrier—the accidents were caused by a minor movement of the stick just prior to touch-down to ensure a 'tailwheel first' landing. In neither case was the aircraft adjudged to be fast by the batsman or by Flyco, but it emphasised the lack of drag possessed by the aircraft. A contributory factor in both instances was that the aircraft was fitted with a 'belly' hook, which gave a hook-to-eye distance significantly smaller than with the more common 'sting' hook.

In the accident where the pilot stalled on the approach, which I witnessed, the aircraft displayed the most graphic example of a 'power on' stall in the Seafire XV. The pilot, in danger of overshooting the turn on the approach, increased his rate of turn to port, with the imminent risk of increasing the aircraft's near-stalled condition. With the Griffon-engine Seafire, a power-on stall would result in a starboard wing drop first and then, if the pilot added power (a natural and instinctive reaction), the torque effect would exaggerate the drop and increase the roll to the right, which could only be made worse by the (again, instinctive) use of aileron to correct the roll instead of by the judicious use of rudder. This is exactly what happened. The pilot attempted to increase his turn to port to line up with the deck and almost immediately flicked and stalled to starboard with no hope of recovery.

Unfortunately, this accident occurred not long after we had arrived in Ceylon. For reasons which still escape me, the Squadron aircraft had been lightered on board from Abbotsinch before leaving Britain instead of being flown on, and there had been no flying for the intervening month until we disembarked the aircraft to Trincomalee. My log book shows a total of only twenty hours' flying in the six weeks from arrival in 'Trinco' to the time of this accident, and it is likely that the pilot concerned, an inexperienced man in his first front-line squadron, would have completed a similar number of hours. An average of seven hours per month over an elapsed period of two and a half months is poor planning by any standards.

Regrettably, the pattern continued at much the same rate throughout the Australian part of the tour. Nor was it only the Seafire squadrons that suffered. The Firefly squadron in *Theseus* (812 NAS) distinguished itself with a series of accidents that could have resulted only from the same lack of flying practice, combined with too much hospitality and too many late nights. Unfortunately it caused more fatalities and the loss of far too many aircraft. Eventually all Air Group flying was suspended on the final day at Sydney until disembarkation to Whanuapai near Auckland, New Zealand, for a period of consolidated flying.

Above and right: No view from the cockpit: two photographs illustrating the well-known incident when Seafire Mk 17 SX333, having landed on board HMS *Triumph* on 30 December 1948, taxied over the barrier and into the forward lift well. The aircraft was a write-off; the pilot no doubt blushed.

The Defining Moment *Commander Graeme Rowan-Thomson*

So it was off to Lossiemouth in Morayshire for Operational Flying School Part I. This was where the RN took over and converted you from the benign training aircraft on to the modern beast, where the engine horsepower was measured in thousands rather than hundreds, and after a brief two hours on a dual-control Firefly you were put into Seafire and told to take off. Those thirty seconds after you had opened the throttle and were dragged into the air behind 2,500 horsepower were, without question, the defining moment in my life—the time when I left my adolescence behind and became a man!

By the time I had raised the undercarriage, trimmed the aircraft and dared to try a gentle turn, I looked out of the cockpit and realised that I had forgotten to throttle back after take-off and Morayshire was unfolding, not far beneath me, at 350 knots. However, I remembered the old adage that every take-off has a landing as well and finally managed to control this missile back on to the ground!

After that we did formation flying, navigation exercises (navexes) and instrument flying, and it was during a navex over the sea that my career—and more—was nearly terminated. This one was done at low level, about 100 feet above the sea, and I was leading a formation of four aircraft, i.e three students and one instructor. It was quite a long haul over the sea and we needed to carry a full drop tank in order to complete the course. To get the fuel in the drop tank flowing into the pipeline there was a changeover lever on the floor of the cockpit so that you could select drop tank or internal fuel supply, and the practice was to select drop tank as soon as you were airborne and then change over to internals some thirty minutes later. There was no gauge to tell you when the tank was running dry.

As leader, I was responsible for the navigation and I was busy checking our position, my course, height, etc., when my engine stopped. I now had a useless propeller windmilling in front of me, and the sea was coming closer. I was just about to wind back the cockpit hood—a prelude to ditching—when my paralysed brain started working again and I leaned down and selected internal fuel. The response was immediate—oodles of lovely power, a propeller spinning like mad and the sea receding beneath me!

When we got back to base and were debriefed by the instructor, he congratulated me on the accuracy of my navigation but said, 'Next time don't fly so low!'

I flew a number of marks of Spitfire as well as the Seafire III and XV and I have never altered my view that it was a superb aeroplane lacking only in sufficient range to compare favourably as a warplane with a number of others—notably the P-51D Mustang. Its ordnance capability also fell short of that of other fighters, for example the Corsair, but in fairness these were of a different timescale. My last flight in a Seafire was in 1950. I came close to flying a Spitfire in 1955, for a delivery flight to the Middle East, but instead had to be content with the delivery of a Provost to Burma!

Big Trouble *Sub-Lieutenant Bernard Pike*

Do you believe in miracles? Has something ever happened in a moment of desperate need that was so extraordinary, so inexplicable and so unbelievable that there just did not seem to be another explanation? I have relived an incident that happened to me during my National Service hundreds if not thousands of times.

It was in December 1953 and I was a nineteen-year-old midshipman who had recently been awarded his 'Wings'. We had been posted to RNAS Yeovilton to join 764 Squadron for OFS Part I, Piston/Fighter, in Seafire 17s. Following just three short dual trips in a Firefly trainer we were away, in what for us was a truly magical experience.

If the Sea Fury that we progressed to later was a Rolls-Royce, then the Seafire was a Mini Cooper. The relatively confined space in its cockpit together with power available and the easy manoeuvrability it offered made the aircraft feel almost an extension of one's own body. This was surely what young men dream about—and, believe me, we dreamt. We were, of course, so fortunate not to be at war and this, to be absolutely honest, was playtime. I am sure that there are people that would pay fortunes for thrills that were but ten per cent of those that came our way.

After a couple of sessions of circuits and bumps, the circuits became a little more assured and the bumps slightly less exaggerated, leading to a sort of straining on the leash by the aces of 764 Squadron. My fourth trip solo was an exercise in area familiarisation, in which we were instructed to visit some well-known local landmarks, the only two that I can now recall being Wincanton Racecourse and that lewd giant carved on a hill near Cerne Abbas. The weather was not brilliant, but who cared? I was living a dream and for the next half hour I really thought that I was God's gift to the world of aviation. It was this foolish belief that almost brought about my end.

In those days, as soon as one had taken off one selected wheels 'up' and changed radio frequency from 'Abel' (airfield) to 'Baker' (district): 'Yeovil Tower, this is Yeovil 130, airborne. Over to Baker. Out.' Having pressed Button B one should then have said, 'Yeovil Tower, this is Yeovil 130, testing. Do you read? Over.' The tower, it was hoped, confirmed that it could hear you—but in my excitement I forgot the test.

I lived only twenty miles from Yeovilton, and as I knew well the landmarks mentioned there did not seem much point in checking them again. Being confident that navigation in this area was not going to be a problem, I ignored instructions and went off on a quick spree up the railway, over to port, and there was my home. A few circuits and a quick pass at max power—but no lower than 1,500 feet—and I could go back to the line that took me to my girlfriend's house, then on to a friend and on to my school, all getting the same treatment. We had been told to stay below cloud, but the gaps seemed huge so I decided to pop up through to see if there was enough space to do a slow roll. The clouds were much higher than I thought and I lost my nerve, so, after flying around for a while, I came back below them again. There was nothing familiar to be seen but—no sweat—I could easily get a homing bearing.

'Yeovil Tower, this is Yeovil 130. Request homing bearing. Over.'

Nothing. I repeated my request.

No answer.

Again and again: 'Yeovil Tower, do you read? Over.'

No reply. My radio sounded alive inasmuch as I could hear myself speaking, but not a squeak was there in return.

My first thought was that I had made some stupid error, and I racked my brains in an effort to discover it. I went back to button 'Abel' and even tried the other frequencies, but without success. During this time I was flying in no particular direction and by now had no idea where I was or what course to set for Yeovilton.

It was slowly dawning on me that I was in big trouble. Our average trip in a Seafire at that time was around an hour, so one could assume that we carried enough fuel for about an hour and twenty minutes, and to my horror I discovered that I had already been airborne for an hour. I can assure you that, in such circumstances, twenty minutes is not a long time

Twenty minutes were soon going to be ten, and decisions had to be made. There were two options: bale out or force-land. To me, sitting in a Seafire without the luxury of an ejection seat, there was no argument: I did not have sufficient pluck to jump out unless the aircraft was actually crashing, and so it had to be a wheels-up forced landing.

I was very scared. Sweating profusely, I prayed: 'Please, God, get me down safely.'

During our time at RAF Syerston, where we learnt to fly, there were lectures (which may have been called 'Air Safety') where problems such as mine were discussed. In a flash I recalled every word and set about putting those lessons into practice. Select your field—large, flat as far as can be ascertained, free from trees and pylons, close to habitation. Check the wind (there was always smoke in view those days) and calculate the approach direction. Reduce speed. Half flap at this time, increasing to full flap on approach. Check that you know where the fuel switch is and be ready to turn it off as soon as you touch down, so as to reduce the risk of fire. Open the hood; tighten the harness. Finally, if you have sufficient fuel, make one or two low circuits to attract attention from the ground should you need assistance.

I carried out all of these tasks and then attempted to transmit one last time what may well be the most useless airborne message ever sent: 'Any Yeovil aircraft, this is Yeovil 130. If you read me, please tell Yeovilton that I am attempting a forced landing in a field.'

I was to learn later that the essence of this had been passed on in a garbled way, and it caused a panic back at base. The Powers That Be had no idea in which direction from Yeovilton I was attempting this precarious undertaking but would have known that my fuel was running out and would have been only too aware that I would shortly be on the ground—somewhere. With my eyes fixed on the chosen field and desperately trying to remember my chosen approach direction, I was, I hoped, being noticed by those on *terra firma*.

Then . . . a miracle!

As I was completing my low-level circuits—which would probably not have been more than a quarter of a mile in diameter—I flew right over the edge of an airfield. What on earth are the odds of an airfield appearing under your wing tip at such a moment?

The runway and the perimeter track had their lights on—which indicates how poor the visibility must have become—and the black and white caravan at the end of the duty

Opposite page: Seafire Mk 17 SX119 when with the Operational Flying School Part I (766 Squadron) at RNAS Lossiemouth in the early 1950s; 764 NAS was re-formed in 1953 out of this unit.
Above and right: Baling-out practice was an essential part of the syllabus for all Seafire trainee pilots. This Mk 17, anchored and trestled, has its engine running, the throttle having been adapted so that it can be controlled by the man standing at the port wing tip, who closes it (via the external cable visible) when the pilot has baled out.

runway was clearly visible. I can offer no explanation as to why I had not seen it earlier. Was it, perhaps, that the lights had only been put on at that moment, as part of the miracle? Had those in the control tower noticed the idiot blundering around at nought feet and realised his predicament? These are questions that I cannot answer.

I waggled my wings over the caravan and, welcome though the green Very light that gave me clearance to land undoubtedly was, nothing was going to stop me coming in now. A rather hairy landing in no way detracted from the truly marvellous feeling that I felt in having got down in one piece. I taxied to the end of the runway, turned back towards the hangars that I could see and then switched off. Flying, I thought, was, perhaps, not for me. Maybe I should retire.

I was sitting in the cockpit and quietly thanking the powers that watch over the foolhardy when two RAF men appeared in a small truck, holding up a blackboard with the chalked instructions 'Follow me'. This was impossible as I needed some power to restart, and when one of them jumped up on the wing he answered my immediate concern by telling me that this was Hullavington, near Bath.

They gave me an undignified ride to the control tower, and as we left my Seafire, with me clutching my parachute and my feet hanging out the back of their truck, I recall noticing that I had forgotten to pick up the flaps. Shown to a small office, I met the most charming, most understanding Flight Lieutenant in the entire Royal Air Force—an older man who, I noted, did not wear a 'Wings' badge.

'Have you been flying Spitfires for long?' he enquired.

He soon realised that I was the novice of all novices and was, to say the least, slightly stressed, so he suggested that a cup of tea might be appropriate.

For the next ten or fifteen minutes we took tea together, and after we had chewed over the differences between Spitfires and Seafires he remarked, casually, 'I suppose we ought to let Yeovilton know where you are.'

A brief telephone conversation followed, and I was told that I would be picked up within the hour. Two instructors arrived in a Firefly trainer (which I could hear long before I could see), one to collect me and the other to pick up my Seafire. As I left it dawned on me that I had not seen another aircraft all the time I had been there.

Back in my crew room, before I even had time to remove my flying overalls, the Chief Flying Instructor looked around the door.

'Pike! You! CO! Now!' he bellowed.

I had no idea what I was about to face. I stood to attention in front of his desk, with the CFI standing behind him.

55

Left: 'Wings Day' at RAF Syerston, 30 October 1953: (front row, left to right) Sub-Lieutenants Bill Box, John Elkin and Alan Bryce, Lieutenant John Brigham and Sub-Lieutenants Dick Perry, Bob Jones, Peter Howard and John Kendal; (back row, left to right) Midshipmen Derek Shorthose, Jim Nightingale, Peter Graham, Peter Nicholson, Ernie Jackson, Bernard Pike, Max Fordham, Michael Baker, Michael Lusty, Peter Taylor, Jim Hopkins, Terry Dewey and John Grierson.

'What the hell do you think you are playing at?' the CO exclaimed.

I tried to assure him that playing was the last thing on my mind, and I went through a sanitised version of the events that had taken place that afternoon. He waved that all aside and then I understood the nature of the real problem.

'You have single-handedly brought chaos to this station today,' he shouted. 'We knew you were down but hadn't a clue where. We calculate that you were on the deck the best part of twenty-five minutes before you had the sense to let us know. We have had to notify police in umpteen counties, had all emergency services standing by, local radio stations have been interrupting programmes asking for information about a lost Seafire, instructors flying all around the area on a wild goose chase looking for an imbecile who has done no more than land at another airfield and has not had the brain to tell us that he is safe. Who met you? Who did you see there?'

I told him about the Flight Lieutenant whose name I did not know, and who had an office on the first floor at the top of the control tower stairs, but I thought it unwise to mention cups of tea. I bent the truth by saying that I thought their tower had informed Yeovilton, but he was unconvinced. He then told the CFI to call Hullavington Tower and try to speak with the Flight Lieutenant. I do not know what was said, but within a short time the whole situation had been defused by that wonderful man with whom I had taken tea. The officers had a few words in private, and then the CO came around my side of his desk and slapped me on the back.

'Good to have you back, son,' he said.

There was probably a sound of relief in his voice, but I took it as a compliment.

My instructor told me later that he believed that a Seafire was a difficult aircraft in which to carry out a wheels-up landing on either land or water, and that my chances of bringing off a successful forced landing with my almost non-existent experience were nil. In his opinion the safer course of action would have been to bale out. As I knew nothing of flying just above the stall, he said, my approach speed would have been far greater than necessary, which would have given the aircraft a nose-down attitude on impact, the low slung radiators of the Seafire would have dug into the turf and I would have cartwheeled on to my back.

Well, it didn't happen!

Right: Against the odds: a successful forced landing by a 'green' pilot flying a Seafire was not entirely unknown, as this photograph of Mk 17 SX365 demonstrates. The pilot, Sub-Lieutenant Peter Howard (here in flying gear with his back to the aircraft), experienced engine failure while taking off from Yeovilton on 16 February 1954 but successfully pulled off a wheels-up landing. His instructor is clasping the inevitable forms.

Speed Trial *Lieutenant-Commander Tom Leece*

The Seafire naval fighter/ground attack aircraft was, without doubt, one of the nicest aeroplanes I have ever flown. I joined the 51st Training Air Group—718 and 719 Squadrons—at RNAS Eglinton for Seafire conversion and operational training in November 1946. We flew principally the Mk III, although a few of the earlier L.IICs were on hand too.

I well remember my first solo. Once I had been strapped in and had started the Merlin, my first impression was of the long engine blocking any forward view, so I raised the seat and started a zig-zag taxi to the runway, did my take-off checks, which included ensuring that the cockpit hood was open, and lined up. The Seafire had a very narrow undercarriage and care had to be taken to control propeller-induced torque, but the acceleration was rapid and the aircraft leapt off the ground. Once airborne, the first thing to do was to brake and raise the undercarriage, and this meant holding the control column with the left hand and reaching down with the right to grasp the very large undercarriage lever, pressing it down out of the 'locked down' notch and swinging it forward to the 'wheels up' position. As I had raised my seat to improve my forward vision for taxying, however, I was now having a little difficulty in retracting the undercarriage—I needed longer arms! All this time the aircraft was accelerating, my left hand was controlling a bucking bronco and my head was too high for me to be able close the hood. Thankfully, it was all sorted out in the end, although the Air Traffic Controller later told me that mine had been one of the liveliest take-offs he had ever seen!

In the operational rôle we used the Seafire not only for air-to-air combat but also for 65-degree dive bombing. This was a very hairy tactic as it felt as though one was descending vertically, and if the ground seemed to be approaching too quickly one had left things too late. We were also trained in ground strafing, low-level bombing, aerial photography and bombardment spotting.

Before completing this training course we had a quick 'scramble' practice. The aircraft were parked in small groups around the perimeter, and when a hooter sounded we jumped in the aircraft, started up and got airborne as quickly as possible, Battle of Britain style. We only did this once but of course we all enjoyed it. On another occasion, during low-level bombing practice, the run-up to the range was over farmland where a farmer was using a horse-drawn device in a field. On the first run he appeared to be shaking his fist at me; on the second run he threw a couple of objects, possibly potatoes, at me that passed just under my wings. I don't blame him: I'd probably have done the same had I been him.

I went on to the deck-landing school at Milltown, a satellite airfield of Lossiemouth in Morayshire. The Seafire was not an easy aeroplane to deck-land: the very qualities that made it such a joy to fly—light and easy control, with swift reaction to the slightest touch—meant that extra care was needed when coming on board a carrier. The narrow-track undercarriage did not help either. I carried out only

Above: Farewell Milltown (HMS *Fulmar II*), 8 November 1951: virtually the 'last hurrah' for the Seafire in RN service and the end of operations at this Station although it was not formally relinquished until 1972. Two Sea Furies are present in the formation flypast, readily identifiable by their less tapering wings. Our contributor Graeme Rowan-Thomson is the port wingman in the centre 'finger-four'; Lieutenant-Commander Hank Henry leads.

thirteen deck landings on Seafire Mk IIIs and XVs (without incident) before we re-equipped with the Mk 47.

The Seafire 47 was the final development of the Spitfire/Seafire line. It was twice the weight of the original Spitfire was fitted with contra-rotating propellers driven by a two-stage, two-speed supercharger in a Griffon engine. The basic aerodynamic shape of the tail section was changed and the end result was a very good, very fast aeroplane. On Feb 24 1948 I carried out a speed trial with a visiting Sea Fury, whose pilot claimed that his new aircraft was the fastest propeller-driven aircraft ever to have been flown. I accepted his challenge to race along the south coast near Brighton. We lined up at 2,000 feet alongside each other and counted down to zero, then opened to full throttle. Initially the Sea Fury pulled ahead, but my Seafire was accelerating all the time and I eventually overtook him.

Another positive feature of the Seafire 47 was its ability to fly high. On 19 April 1948 I was detailed to carry out an oxygen climb to an altitude above 40,000 feet. I managed 40,500 on the altimeter and contacted RNAS Ford to report my position and height—which I did with difficulty as I had hardly sufficient air in my lungs to pronounce the words.

I also had a ten-minute flight in a Seafire 46, a five-bladed aircraft with a high-torque problem at slow speeds. My flight lasted for only ten minutes—'for technical reasons'!

SEAFIRE AT WAR–1

Rear-Admiral Ray Rawbone CB AFC

THE Spitfire was designed to defend our cities, and its main rôle was to gain air supremacy in air-to-air combat. It was so successful that it became a legend in its time. So much has been written about it that it is difficult to add to the story. With minimum modification the Seafire was adapted to meet the requirements of Fleet Air Arm's squadrons at sea. Its main rôle remained that of air defence (now, of course, of the Fleet), but very little seems to have been written about the many and varied secondary rôles for which this amazingly versatile aircraft was used. With this in mind, and with the aid of my diary kept in 1944, I thought it would be of interest to record events as I remember them in a Seafire squadron during the last two years of the war. Unfortunately my diary does not extend into 1945, and so my dates and details in that year are based on log book records.

809 Squadron was a typical Naval Squadron, and I believe its service both at sea and ashore clearly illustrates the flexibility and effective operation of this great aircraft during the final two years of World War II. New-entry pilots were as well trained as was possible in a country at war, and it is interesting to note that those volunteering to join the Fleet Air Arm in 1941 had to wait about eight months before being called up to commence training.

* * *

I recall a wonderful day in the summer of 1941. After the desperate days of Dunkirk and the apprehension during the Battle of Britain, we saw Alex Henshaw, the Chief Test Pilot of Vickers at Castle Bromwich, give a dazzling display of aerobatics in a Spitfire, flying inverted along the streets of Birmingham and thoroughly demonstrating the true qualities of a great aircraft. I understand that not all the city councillors were pleased, but it was a real boost for the public and a great inspiration for the many youngsters waiting to be called into the Services for aircrew training.

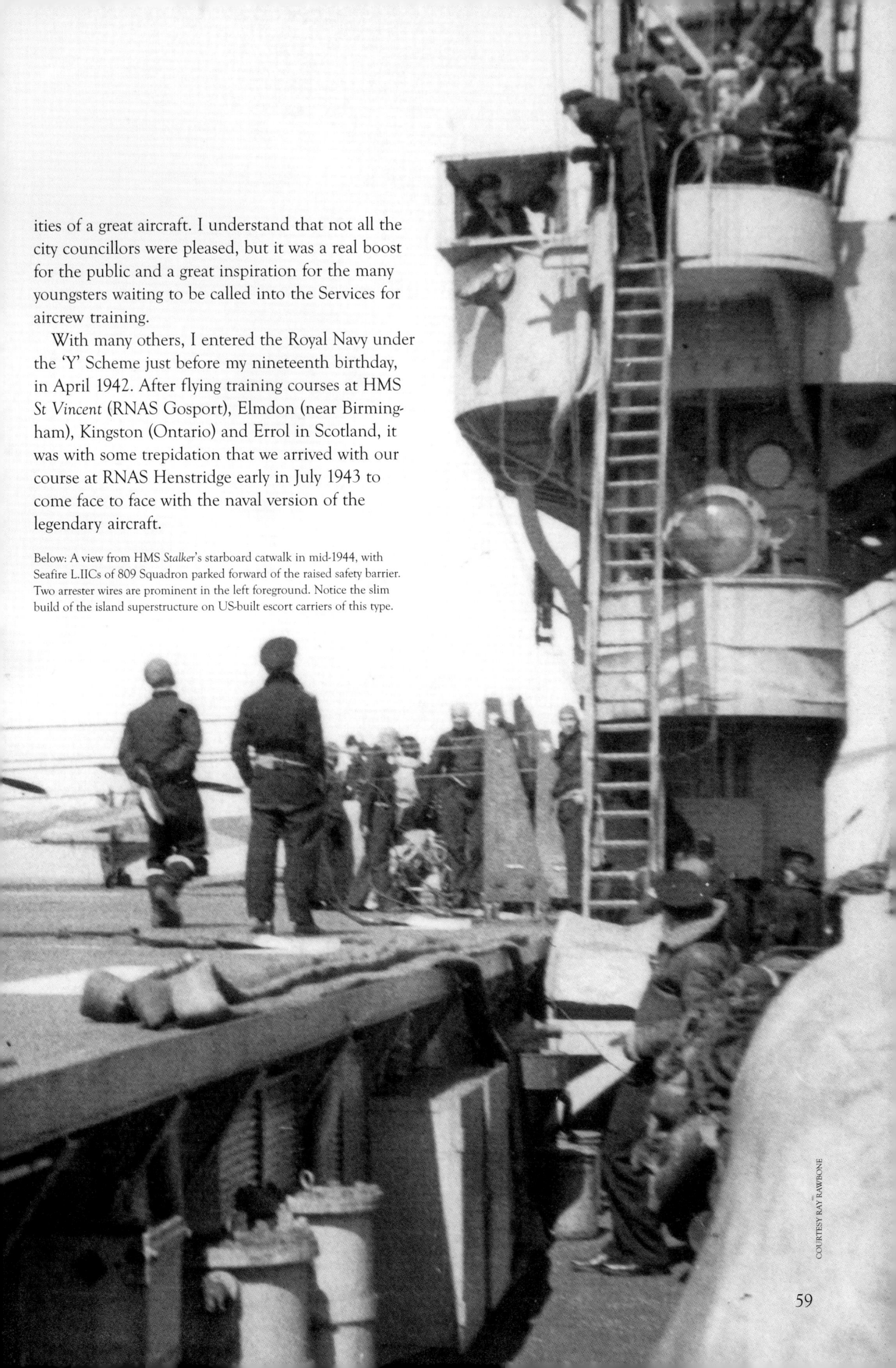

With many others, I entered the Royal Navy under the 'Y' Scheme just before my nineteenth birthday, in April 1942. After flying training courses at HMS *St Vincent* (RNAS Gosport), Elmdon (near Birmingham), Kingston (Ontario) and Errol in Scotland, it was with some trepidation that we arrived with our course at RNAS Henstridge early in July 1943 to come face to face with the naval version of the legendary aircraft.

Below: A view from HMS *Stalker*'s starboard catwalk in mid-1944, with Seafire L.IICs of 809 Squadron parked forward of the raised safety barrier. Two arrester wires are prominent in the left foreground. Notice the slim build of the island superstructure on US-built escort carriers of this type.

The operational training unit was equipped with the Seafire IB, which certainly lived up to all our expectations. It was a snug aircraft to fit into and the pilot felt part of the machine. The Merlin 45 engine was powerful, smooth and responsive, and control at all speeds was excellent. Above all, the pilot felt that he was in an aircraft which could match anything an enemy could put up against him.

The 55-hour operational course was centred on air-to-air combat but finished with a concentrated period of dummy deck landings in preparation for embarkation in HMS *Argus* and final deck landing qualification. I am sure that we all considered this to be our most formidable challenge.

The Seafire had limited forward visibility when trimmed in the approach attitude, and a curved final approach was essential. The cockpit hood was opened and held back by a notched door: forget this part of the drill and you could receive a painful reminder as the hood slid rapidly forward when catching a wire. We didn't have bone domes then!

Unfortunately, the Seafire's undercarriage was a weak link: it was not designed to absorb continuous heavy duty on an aircraft carrier's deck. Nevertheless, this disadvantage was offset to a large extent by very responsive control even at low approach speeds a few knots above a stalling speed of about 58 knots. Its beautifully designed shape also demanded firm control of the final approach speed. Too fast and the aircraft would almost certainly float over the arrester wires and into the barrier—or occasionally over the barrier and into the deck park!

There was much to think about as we joined HMS *Argus*. She was an old, straight-deck carrier with four non-centering wires and a small retractable bridge. Operating in Scottish waters near Ailsa Craig, she was our first introduction to the real world at sea. A similar course from Yeovilton, flying Hurricanes, was already embarked. We watched enthralled as one Hurricane went over the side, a second went over the side but was retained by its hook, a third damaged its undercarriage slightly and a fourth made a perfect landing! No one was hurt and it was an exciting display, but it did not leave us brimming with confidence!

A first deck landing is forever etched in every Naval pilot's mind. In my debrief I was firmly told that I had received every signal in the book; I was just thankful to be safely on deck with no A25 (accident report) to fill. Much to our relief, the whole course qualified with four deck landings each and we disembarked to join operational squadrons shortly afterwards. It was hard to believe that we had come

Below: New Seafire L.IICs of 809 Squadron nestle in *Stalker*'s hangar, their paintwork gleaming in the artificial light. Stowage efficiency is compromised by the fact that these aircraft cannot fold their wings; this would change when the Seafire Mk III was issued to the Squadron. HMS *Stalker* was one of eleven *Attacker* class escort carriers taken into service by the Royal Navy. They displaced some 10,500 tons (standard) and could make 18 knots.

Above: HMS *Stalker* en route to Gibraltar in August 1943, when her air group comprised 880 Squadron plus a flight from 833, together with, here, a pair of Grumman Martlets for delivery to other units. The Seafires are a mixture of Mk IICs (three-bladed propellers) and L. Mk IICs (four-bladed), and several have had their wing tips removed. The carrier was on her way to take part in Operation 'Avalanche', the landings at Salerno.

so far in eighteen months and that we were now entrusted to fly Mitchell's great aircraft in action.

809 Squadron and HMS *Stalker*

Together with George Fry, a Southern Irishman, I joined 809 Squadron based at Andover in October 1943. We were to remain with the Squadron until it decommissioned at the end of the war.

Our base was a very large grass field on the edge of a major road which is now the A303. We were equipped with twenty-four Seafires, initially a mixture of Mk IICs (Merlin 46) and L. Mk IICs (Merlin 32), commanded by Major Al Wright RM, a smart, rather strict disciplinarian—which was probably just as well as we had a fair mixture of high-spirited Commonwealth officers!

Our parent carrier, HMS *Stalker*, was a typical American-built ship supplied on Lease-Lend to the Royal Navy and one of three carriers which normally operated in company, the other two being HMS *Attacker* (879 Squadron) and HMS *Hunter* (807 Squadron). Each carrier could accommodate twenty-four Seafires with an additional three or four aircraft in reserve.

On joining the Squadron we learnt that the three carriers had just returned from Salerno, where very low wind speeds over the decks had resulted in very many deck-landing accidents, which, with battle damage taken into account, had led to an exceptionally high attrition rate overall. After the battle it had been alleged that only three or four serviceable Seafires in total remained among the three carriers. We were lucky, therefore, to receive an increasing number of new L.IICs as we re-equipped—a lovely aircraft, especially at low level, and, in my opinion, one of the best marks of Seafire ever to enter Naval service. We soon discovered that there were many more rôles to master than air combat. Under the watchful eye of our experienced pilots, much greater emphasis was placed on ground attack, tactical reconnaissance, army support, air-to-ground photography, spotting for the artillery and low-level bombing. Both pilot and aircraft needed to be truly versatile to make a fair fist of the many requirements.

We worked hard for the next three months, cramming in as many hours as possible. Great emphasis was placed on low-level pilot navigation as it was considered essential to keep as low as possible in order to avoid detection by enemy radar and other early-warning devices. This was a tactic that we thoroughly enjoyed at the time but one we quickly abandoned some nine months later when temporarily attached to RAF squadrons in Italy and faced with very heavy and accurate German flak.

Immediately after Christmas 1943 we embarked in our parent carrier for a month's familiarisation. During this period George Fry went over the side whilst landing. He was quickly rescued by seaboat and brought alongside but, unfortunately, wet and bedraggled, he was struck on the head by the hoisting tackle as the seaboat arrived inboard. George was not amused, and the ship's Executive Commander, who was supervising the rescue, was subjected to a good old Irish dressing-down by an outraged sub-lieutenant! It was, however, all in a day's work and quickly forgotten.

During the next three months we continued our work-up, which included disembarkation in turn to Dale, Eglinton and Long Kesh (near Belfast) for live weapon training, and on 1 May 1944, whilst at Long Kesh, we were given a few hours' notice to re-embark for our first operation, a strike against enemy shipping off Norway. Fresh eggs were a luxury at the time and there were plenty in Ireland. We had all stocked up with a couple of dozen each, and, with minimum packaging in which to carry them, we had no option but to place them carefully in the Seafires' wing ammunition containers and hope for the best. With great concentration we all landed on board safely . . . and not an egg was broken. You have to get your priorities right!

A few days later, on the eve of the strike, we were recalled to the Irish Sea. No explanation was given, but we soon found ourselves in company with HMS *Attacker* and HMS *Hunter*, escorting a very large convoy to Gibraltar. Previous convoys had been subjected to continuous shadowing by German long-range Focke-Wulf Condors with the inevitable risk of U-boat interception, but we did not see a single enemy aircraft—which was hardly surprising as we flew continuous patrols of at least four Seafires in daylight hours and had some seventy-two aircraft in total upon which to call.

Having disembarked some aircraft to North Front, the carriers berthed inside Gibraltar harbour, which was just as well as imminent air raids were expected. In consequence we spent the third night strapped in our aircraft in two-hour shifts at immediate readiness to scramble and intercept any incoming enemy raiders. This was exciting, but it was viewed with some anxiety since we all had scant experience of night flying and we were well aware of the difficulties of landing the early marks of Seafire at night because of the glare from the exhausts on final approach. Fortunately, we were let off the hook as there was no air attack and no one was scrambled. There was, however, a large explosion on the seaward side of the western mole right opposite the point where *Attacker* was berthed. This was eventually alleged to have been the work of underwater Italian swimmers based across the bay near Algeçiras. We did not realise it at the time, but it is now clear that our carriers were all part of the build-up of forces in readiness for Operation 'Dragoon', the invasion of the South of France.

War in the Mediterranean

Early in June 809 Squadron flew via Oran to Blida, an RAF base in Algeria. We were accommodated in a tented camp with minimum facilities. However, our maintenance crews responded with their usual cheerful efficiency and we continued an intensive flying programme, alternating between ship and shore and integrating with other naval units and the Army and RAF as the situation required. It soon became obvious that the Allies had complete air superiority in the area, and no enemy aircraft were sighted. We were, however, frequently 'bounced' by the Group Captain and Wing Commander—both Battle of Britain pilots—and we quickly learned to defend ourselves.

On 15 June we suffered our first fatal casualty when Lieutenant Tyson Davidson stalled on his final approach to land on board *Stalker* and flew into the round-down—a tragic introduction to the hard facts of life in the war at sea. In the very light winds encountered we became used to the many relatively minor deck landing accidents that occurred, but we were shaken by two major incidents a few weeks before 'D-Day' in the South of France. In each case the pilot concerned missed both wires and barriers and landed in the deck park, writing off or damaging twelve aircraft all in two days—a major blow-out of a complement of twenty-four aircraft at a very critical time.

We were used to a logistic run along the staging airfields in North Africa between Bône and Blida and between Blida and Gibraltar but I am not sure how HMS *Stalker* dealt with the replenishment of so many aircraft. She did so, however—and, clearly, during the time we were disembarked at Blida. These accidents were also a forceful reminder to pilots to vacate their cockpits quickly having landed on and switched off in the deck park!

Being a nose-heavy aircraft, the Seafire was inclined to 'peck' its propeller when catching a wire on landing. In light winds, damage to propellers increased alarmingly, and a lack of spares threatened to ground aircraft. During initial training we had all been impressed when, during a visit to Rolls-Royce, it was demonstrated how each propeller was finely balanced—the weight of a cigarette paper could turn a propeller on a free axis—and we were therefore mesmerised when our Squadron AEO appeared on deck to saw two inches off each propeller blade in an effort to reduce accidental damage. It did work, and the Seafire performed splendidly.

Opposite page: *Stalker* had a theoretical aircraft capacity of twenty, but the non-folding Seafire reduced this complement and, indeed, the ship always had to accommodate a proportion of her aircraft topside. Here some of her Seafire L.IICs, now well weathered, are seen ranged to starboard so as to provide the maximum flight-deck width possible for continuing air operations. The ship had two lifts for access to the hangar; that aft is clearly visible. Right: Seafire MB267 comes to grief in *Stalker*'s barrier, having apparently missed the wires; the pilot is being assisted from his cockpit. The aircraft, which is a Mk IIC that has been modified by having its wing tips clipped, appears to have been re-engined, and this photograph demonstrates that the number of exhaust outlets (six per side *versus* three) is not, on its own, a reliable identifying feature as to the mark of Seafire depicted.

Above: A beaming Lieutenant David Lees-Jones in the cockpit of his Seafire. This 809 Squadron pilot was destined to lose his life in particularly tragic circumstances, as related by the writer on page 81.

Increased emphasis was placed on low-level dive-bombing techniques, usually with delayed-action fuses. With a live bomb on board and in light wind conditions over the decks, the Seafire needed fifteen degrees of flap to increase lift on take-off. As flap could only be selected fully up or fully down, an intermediate fifteen degrees was achieved by trapping a wooden wedge within the flaps before take-off. Once the aircraft was safely airborne the flaps were selected to the fully down position and the wooden blocks each side would fall out, allowing the pilot to retract the flaps and climb away. This 'fix' worked well, and I cannot remember any asymmetric malfunction which would have severely curtailed the number of bombing missions.

With the Royal Air Force

Early in May Lieutenant-Commander Eaden relieved Al Wright as Commanding Officer, and there were further changes of personnel over the next two months. In July it was decided that a number of pilots from each squadron (809, 807 and 879) should be deployed to join selected RAF fighter squadrons on the front line in Italy, and on 11 July I joined our Senior Pilot, Lieutenant David Ogle, in a flight from Blida to Castilione in Italy to take up a week's attachment to No 208 Squadron, then based near Lake Trasimeno. No 208 shared the airfield with No 40 Squadron SAAF and were equipped with Spitfires. Their main task was armed reconnaissance and army support, and each day they were heavily

Left: The writer in informal pose in the cockpit of his Seafire. It can be deduced from this photograph, and from that above, that the Seafire pilot's headroom was not exactly generous.
Opposite page: A fitter attends to a Seafire's starboard oblique F.24 camera—the essential tool for an armed reconnaissance sortie.

backed up by a 'cab rank' of Allied fighter-bombers, principally Mustangs.

We were warmly welcomed and quickly absorbed into their operational schedules. For the first two or three sorties, as an introduction to the heavy German flak, we acted as 'weavers' for the recce pilots. Our low-flying techniques were quickly abandoned, as 40mm flak was intense up to 4,000 feet and 88mm flak very accurate around 8,000. We flew at about 6,000 feet, constantly weaving and changing direction. We flew two or three sorties a day either on reconnaissance missions or spotting for the Army's heavy guns. A very enthusiastic army liaison officer decided that it would be 'beneficial' if some pilots could visit Army personnel in the front line to gain a 'better feel' for those actually firing the guns. It was a little unnerving for the inexperienced as we crept to within 600 yards of the enemy positions, but we came away very impressed with the demeanour and discipline of the soldiers in the front line. Needless to say, we were even more impressed when we retired to a safe distance for a picnic lunch complete with some of the regimental silver!

On three occasions while acting as a recce pilot I found columns of MT (motor transport) and, having made my report, was surprised how quickly the 'cab rank' reacted to it. On my last flight I found forty MT in a defile south of Cagli and twenty tanks in Cagli itself. In order to try and identify the targets I flew rather too close for comfort and was forced to make a rapid retreat! The flak was so heavy the sky seemed to be full of tracer and explosives. I didn't envy the pilots of the Mustangs called in to bomb and rocket the targets!

On 18 July, after a week in which we learnt a great deal about interdiction and front-line army support operations, we said goodbye to No 208 Squadron and flew back to re-join our squadron at Blida. Three days later we re-embarked in *Stalker*, although, as Arch Foley had crashed in Italy, Graham Moore had caught malaria and Lex Aspinall had been reappointed, we went on board with only seventeen pilots.

Stalker was now operating within the area between Malta and North Africa and we soon found ourselves in company with three other carriers—HMS *Hunter*, USS *Kasaan Bay* (CVE-69) and USS *Tulagi* (CVE-72)—and under the command of an American Admiral. A short excursion to Alexandria and a return to Malta allowed time to exercise together and to standardise routines and communications. We also began to receive some Seafire L.IIIs (Merlin 55) as replacements for damaged L.IICs. During this period Leading Naval Airman (Photographer) Eddie Wood was able to photograph a spectacular crash as Ted Stephenson went over the side on landing and nose-dived into the sea. At the time, Eddie was photographing Ralph Barker, who had just crash-landed and was hanging over the catwalk. Both pilots were unhurt. Eddie later became a photographer for the *Western Evening Post* and the *Western Daily Press*.

Operation 'Dragoon'

On 12 August 1944 we all sailed to support the invasion of the South of France, centred on the area of St-Raphael and St-Tropez, with Toulon and Marseilles the main objectives. As we approached our operating area about 60-70 miles south of the French coast, we found ourselves part of a task force of nine aircraft carriers, *Hunter*, *Stalker*, *Attacker*, *Tulagi*, *Kasaan Bay*, HMS *Pursuer*, HMS *Khedive*, HMS *Emperor* and HMS *Searcher*, all adequately supported by escorts and replenishment ships.

'D-Day', 15 August. Overnight, Allied commandos and paratroops had captured the Île de Levant and landed in mainland France. Ships went to Action Stations at about 0530 and, as dawn broke, the Commanding Officer's flight, including our Wing Leader, Lieutenant-Commander Hallett, was launched to spot for ships taking part in the initial bombardment. The sea was flat calm and the wind over the deck was never more than 20 knots, and in

hazy conditions visibility was poor. At 0655 our flight took off to provide CAP for the fleet. The sky was full of Allied heavy bombers—an estimated 400-500 during our patrol—but no enemy aircraft were seen or reported.

My next mission was in support of bombarding ships, but I was unable to get a target from the Air Controller. Together with my wingman, Sub-Lieutenant John Brittain, I made a recce inland over two German-occupied towns, Grimaud and Cogolin. There was a complete lack of enemy movement and ack-ack, and the towns seemed deserted. There were hundreds of landing barges and ships along the coast as we set course for *Stalker*. Visibility was bad. As our YG direction beacons were not working and our fuel state was low, we were worried in case we missed the

Left, top: One of HMS *Khedive*'s Seafires, armed with a 500-pound bomb under its belly, takes off for a strike during Operation 'Dragoon'. The red-painted fuselage codes, hardly visible in monochrome, read 'K-4'.

Left, bottom: Ralph Barker's deck-landing mishap on board *Stalker*, his L.IIC, fortuitously, having been caught on the port catwalk before it disappeared into the water below.

Right: Another view of Ralph Barker's unconventional deck-landing; he was, fortunately, unhurt. The 'prang' has severely damaged one of the ship's 20mm Oerlikon mountings.

Below, right: As described on page 65, while LNA(P) Eddie Wood was in the process of photographing Ralph Barker's 'prang' another Seafire, piloted by Ted Stephenson, was involved in a deck-landing accident and shot over the side into the sea—as shown here. Fortunately, the pilot escaped from this mishap too. One of the three carriers accompanying *Stalker* is dimly discernible on the horizon.

force. However we landed on safely and shortly after were airborne again on CAP.

Overall, it had been a successful day for the invasion force but a surprisingly quiet one for the Squadron. We did have two pilots who went into the barriers on landing, and Sub-Lieutenant George Morris had to ditch when he ran out of fuel having lost the force. George landed about a mile from an air–sea rescue launch, which unfortunately did not see him. Eventually realising that he was not going to be picked up, George, a very strong swimmer, took off his Mae West and swam to the launch! He was returned to us the next day. Two of *Pursuer*'s pilots baled out.

'D + 1', 16 August. As Allied forces moved inland, the Squadron had a day of mixed tasks, providing cover for the task force and fighter-bomber sorties against German road and rail communications. We carried 250-pound bombs and attacked rail and road junctions to the north-east of Toulon. Three trains were destroyed and MT and armoured cars were strafed and scattered along the roads.

After our last sortie it was nearly dark when we landed on, and Lieutenant Tony Fradd used illuminated bats to bring us to the deck. Wind speed over the deck was low, but we all landed safely with the exception of John Brittain, who unfortunately landed short; his tail hit the round-down and the aircraft's back was broken. John was unhurt. The two pilots from *Pursuer* were picked up safely and returned to their ship.

'D + 2', 17 August. An early fighter-bomber sortie of six aircraft attacked and damaged a road and rail bridge, but otherwise it was a quiet day of combat air patrols over the task force and beaches. Nothing was seen.

'D + 3', 18 August. A quiet morning providing beach and force cover. As the German forces were driven north away from the coast, we were given more inter-

67

diction targets and four of our aircraft found a small armoured column and strafed it to a standstill. I flew in the Senior Pilot's flight, and, heading towards the coast, we were tasked to attack two large barges used by the Germans as ferries for heavy equipment and troop movements. They were heavily armed with 40mm and 88mm flak, as we soon discovered.

We pressed home our attack with cannon and machine guns until both barges were stopped and badly damaged. David James reported that he had been hit but was able to continue as we flew inland on an armed recce mission. Flying alongside David, we could see no obvious damage, but as he was returning to land on, his airspeed indicator and other instruments began to malfunction. Nevertheless, he made a perfect landing with a very large hole inside his port mainplane, brought about by an exploding 40mm shell.

'D + 4', 19 August. The Squadron was heavily tasked on armed recce, photo recce and dive-bombing missions. Early on, David James's aircraft was badly hit by flak while diving on an armed recce sortie. He managed to reach the sea before baling out. After three-quarters of an hour he was picked up unhurt by a destroyer.

Elements of a panzer division had been reported in the Nîmes area and David Ogle and myself each led flights to try to locate them. David's aircraft and mine were each fitted with F.24 cameras and we were tasked with taking oblique photographs of enemy dispositions. David covered the area between Narbonne and Montpellier and I took the area between Nîmes and Montpellier. The two barges strafed the night before were seen beached and abandoned on the coast.

Nîmes railway junction and the adjacent airfield were photographed, but little movement was seen although the area was solid with flak. On the road between Nîmes and Montpellier, elements of an armoured division were stretched out at intervals, including some tanks. They were photographed and reported to the Air Controller.

Close by on the railway we found a long train carrying MT and armoured vehicles, possibly tanks. We strafed the train until it burst into flames, and as the last aircraft in the flight finished its run I flew in at 500 feet to photograph the damage. A big mistake! I was suddenly shocked by a machine gun or cannon strike which split part of my windscreen frame from the airframe about two feet in front of my face! A steep climb and an instinctive desire to stay alive took me to a safe height from which to take the photographs. David Ogle also reported armoured columns in the area.

Below: A map of the South of France showing Admiral Rawbone's area of operations during his participation in Operation 'Dragoon', August–September 1944.

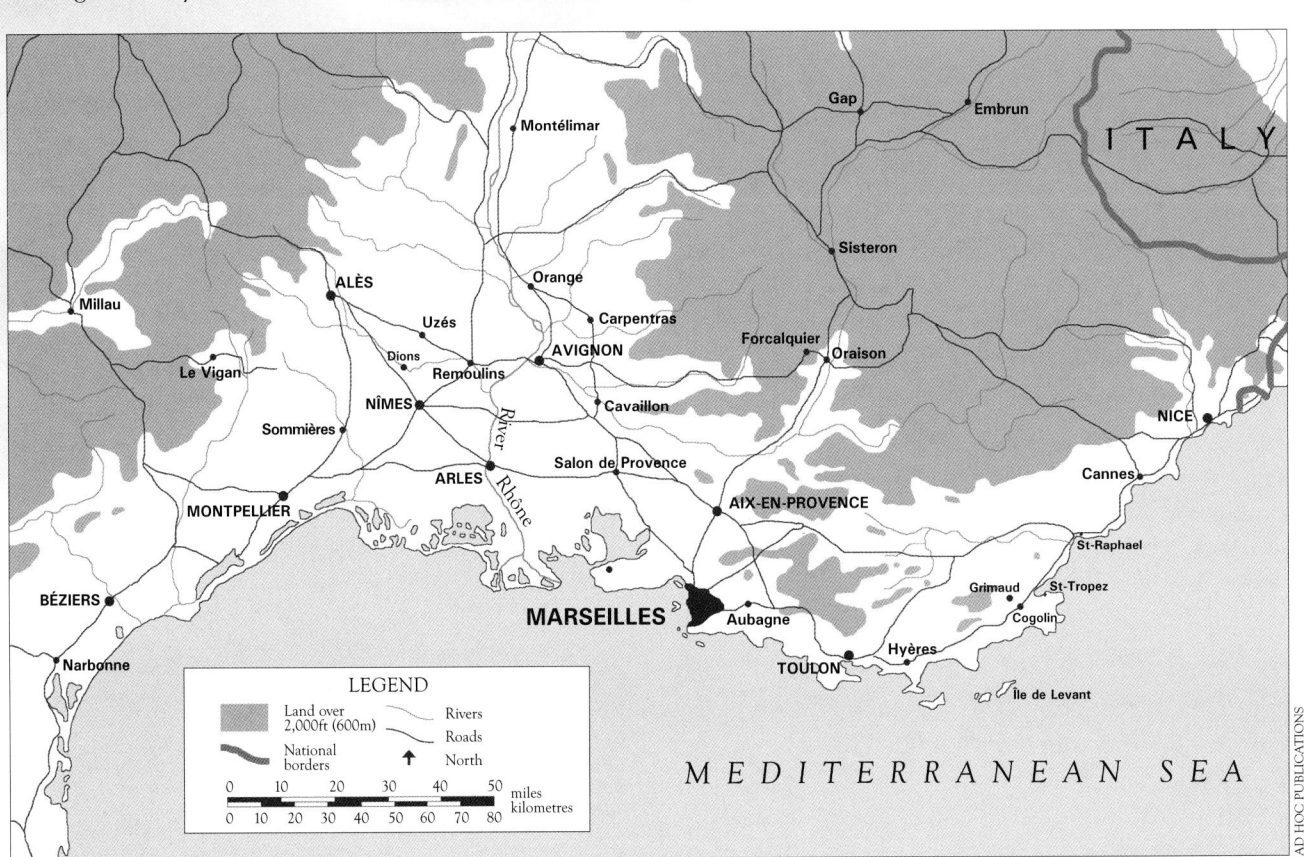

Above: Fire was always a possibility following a deck-landing accident, but the threat was efficiently dealt with by HMS *Khedive*'s fire crews following a 'prang' by this Seafire L.IIC during the 'Dragoon' operations.

Later in the day, Squadron aircraft strafed and destroyed several MT and staff cars and set four trains on fire. Tony Perry's aircraft was hit but he made a wonderful flapless landing on board in low wind conditions.

'D + 5', 20 August. A day mostly spent spotting for American warships directing their guns against coastal batteries in the Toulon area. I was detailed to work with the battleship *Nevada*. We had to wait for a target but eventually the ship decided to engage a coastal battery of eight guns. At first I underestimated the range and fall of shot, but the adjustments made to bracket the target were meticulously followed and we soon had five or six 14-inch shells landing right on target. It must have been the Americans' first engagement as they were very excited and asked for a full report after each salvo. With small, accurate adjustments the ship damaged or destroyed every gun pit and set most on fire. When I left it also looked as though a large ammunition store was ablaze.

'D + 6', 21 August. A very busy day. We all flew sorties, dive-bombing and strafing German transport trying to move northwards up the Rhône valley. We were airborne at first light to dive-bomb a railhead north of Nîmes. On a later sortie I flew with our Flight Commander, Jeff Jefferson, to attack MT columns in the area of Uzés. We found our first column just moving out of town and immediately engaged with cannon and machine guns. We found a second column shortly afterwards and strafed its vehicles until we had exhausted our ammunition. In each case the flak was light and we had many hits but surprisingly only three or four flamers. On the way back to *Stalker*, almost every Allied aircraft seemed to be in the sky and any German movement must have been well and truly pounded!

Having landed the Squadron on, *Stalker* left the area for a two-day break and rest at Maddalena. As always, this was an opportunity for our maintenance crews under Flight Sergeant 'Tammy' Walker to set to and carry out vital aircraft maintenance and repairs. It was also an essential break for the ship's company and flight-deck crews in which to catch up on a backlog of work and keep the ship running smoothly ready for the next round of operations. The aircrew probably were best placed to enjoy any rest period!

'D + 9', 24 August. A date firmly etched in my memory! Back in the operating area Lieutenant Jefferson's flight was airborne at 0640 to carry out a tactical recce of the Nîmes-Rhône area. We were a flight of three aircraft as my Number Two was unserviceable on the flight deck and did not take off.

Just after 0715 I was temporarily detached to check the roads west of Nîmes. At 0725 I saw a German staff car proceeding north towards Arles. I attacked, and a heavy group of cannon shells brought the car to a standstill. I saw no further movement and at 0730 turned south towards Nîmes to rendezvous with Lieutenant Jefferson. A few moments later I noticed that the engine was running very roughly. The boost pressure dropped off and twelve-inch flames appeared from the exhausts. The maximum revs attainable were 2,200. I decided to get as far south as possible, hoping to reach the sea or Allied troops. I was then at 4,000 feet. I gave my tac-recce report to my Flight Commander and reported my condition over RTF.

At 800 feet, about seven miles west of Nîmes, my engine cut out and I prepared to land in two small fields; it was not easy to bale out of a Seafire, and I was clearly too low. My instruments began to malfunction and the air speed indicator stopped working. However, the aircraft still handled well enough to judge the final approach by feel. I landed just short of the fields, finishing up amongst bushes and trees in a small clearing. My R/T was still working and I was able to contact Lieutenant Jefferson, giving my position and telling him that I was unhurt. I had landed between the Nîmes-Arles and Nîmes-Montpellier roads, five miles west of Nîmes.

As a pocket on my gloves contained coded information, I placed the gloves in the cockpit together with my helmet and set fire to the aircraft with the small incendiary bomb provided. There was a small explosion; I saw smoke from the resulting blaze whilst still in the area an hour later. At this stage I saw several men, whom I took to be Germans, about 800 yards away and heading towards the aircraft from the west. I took my emergency rations and knife from my Mae West before hiding it in thick scrub and running off swiftly in the opposite direction! About a mile from the aircraft I thought it prudent to hide from several French people who were making for the crash.

After hiding for an hour I moved north around Nîmes before turning eastwards towards more rugged territory, where I felt sure I would find help from French farmers or from the *Maquis*. Crossing the main Nîmes-Arles road was hazardous, but, having crossed it safely, I walked about six miles before risking contact with a lone Frenchman working in a field. I had some trouble persuading him that I was English and not German, but, once satisfied, he quickly took me to his home in the village of Dions. One of his family was a member of the *Maquis*, and after a meal I was introduced to a young lady who spoke English.

Dions lies on a secondary road much used by the Germans to transport their troops from Montpellier to Uzés. I was therefore advised to stay put for a few days, until the Allies had reached and crossed the Rhône. The young lady's parents owned a large farm and without hesitation offered to take me in, sharing my nightly accommodation alternatively with the first family. Early warning of German transit movements was provided by the *Maquis* so that I could hide elsewhere as necessary. The adrenalin flowed for the next two days as two columns of German MT passed through the village and I hid in a small copse nearby. The first column of eight mixed trucks was ambushed half a mile from the village by the *Maquis*. Four Hellcats joined the fray with heavy strafing, and the damage was devastating. The second column of sixty vehicles, which included some tanks, was sighted by Allied aircraft as it approached Uzés and the sound of explosions and cannon-fire indicated that it had been immediately engaged.

The following day the village was quiet but the *Maquis* appeared to be everywhere. They liberated Nîmes on 27 August and quickly cleared the approach roads. On the 28th I left Dions with three French friends and cycled into Nîmes—an exciting journey as we did not know what to expect. I was quickly passed to Major Sharpe of the Special Forces working with the *Maquis*, who arranged motorcycle passage to Arles, where I crossed the Rhône by rowing boat, and on 30 August I made contact with Lieutenant-Colonel White, an English liaison officer with a French division. That day I re-crossed the Rhône with the division, and they took me with them as they advances to Uzés. The following morning, 31 August, I was flown by Piper Cub to the air base at Salon.

During the time spent on the move I had seen many examples of the carnage caused by cannon and machine-gun strafing. This had been militarily effective and essential, but it also clearly brought to mind the horrific tragedies that had been faced by many helpless civilian families as they struggled to escape along the main transport routes during the early *Blitzkrieg* days of the war. War is not glamorous if one is on the receiving end.

From Salon I was flown to Naples, and I quickly learnt that the carriers had been withdrawn from the South of France and that HMS *Stalker* was en route to Alexandria. I was very anxious to get back to the ship as soon as possible as I knew that my drama was being shared by my family at home and I had no idea of their state of mind nor the detail of any information passed to them. My wife was expecting our first child, and it must have been a great shock for her to open a telegram reporting that I was missing. Fortunately a second communication arrived the same day, Lieutenant Jefferson having received my message that I was unhurt and having seen me leave the aircraft at some speed! I quickly made contact with the family from Naples. We were all conscious that our families also served as they patiently remained at home and dutifully waited for news. I took passage to Malta by air and the next day flew to Cairo. From Cairo I had a lift by car to Alexandria, and arrived on board *Stalker* at 2000 on the 7 September.

I had been lucky. The gods must have been with me, but some bad news awaited. Lieutenant Jefferson had been killed on 26 August whilst attacking a German column near St-Remy; his wing had been shot off by flak at low level and he had had no chance to bale out. This was a further blow for me as I had great respect and admiration for my Flight Commander. Sub-Lieutenant Macnamee, who had recently joined the Squadron, had also been killed. He had released his bomb at too low a level whilst dive-bombing and the resultant blast had caused fatal damage to his aircraft.

The Greek Islands and the Aegean
Whilst HMS *Stalker* was in Alexandria harbour the Squadron was disembarked to Dekheila airfield. On 18 September we flew on board again and sailed in company with the light cruiser HMS *Black Prince* and two destroyers heading for Greek waters. Our mission was to provide cover for our minesweepers

Left: Combat air patrol: Seafire L.IICs of 807 Squadron about to take off from HMS *Hunter* during Operation 'Dragoon'. Although the *Attacker* class escort carriers were equipped with a single catapult (at the port bow), this was rarely employed when a mass strike or a mass patrol was being flown off.

71

operating in channels around the islands and to take offensive action against German movements of air, sea, road and rail transport in and Greece amongst the main islands in the surrounding area.

From 26 to 29 September 809 Squadron covered our minesweepers sweeping a channel off Amorges island and carried out extensive reconnaissance of the area. Shipping in the harbour north of Leros and in Siros was attacked with 500-pound bombs. Five ferries were damaged at sea and were finally destroyed by one of our destroyers. The CO's flight caught and destroyed a Ju 52 landing at Rhodes and set fire to a small column of German MT approaching the airfield.

On 28 September we sailed north through the swept channel for a short period before leaving the area on the 29th and returning to Alexandria. During this period Sub-Lieutenant Davis hit the round-down on landing and wrote off his aircraft; Sub-Lieutenant John Brittain was waved off just before touch-down, his engine cut but he managed to drop on the deck, damaging both oleos and a wing. The Squadron also suffered another minor accident and there were two barrier landings. None of the pilots was hurt.

On 5 October, in company with HMS *Hunter*, we left Alexandria and sailed through the swept channels into the Aegean Sea. After further reconnaissance we sank two merchant ships with 500-pound bombs and forced a flak ship to beach. On 7 October Tony Perry and George Morris strafed a German MT column on the island of Cos, but, sadly, Tony was shot down and crashed in flames about 400 yards beyond his target.

During the next few days we moved further north to give cover to the cruisers *Black Prince* and *Aurora*, which had re-joined our force after a sortie in the Salonika area. Together with 807 Squadron (HMS *Hunter*), we attacked and destroyed several trains in Greece and to the west of Salonika, and signal boxes, water towers and rail junctions were attacked in order to disrupt the Germans' mobility. Enemy ships and ferries were attacked on sight. The CO bombed and scored a direct hit on a destroyer.

The flak was generally moderate except around Larissa airfield, rail junctions and large ferries, where 40mm and 88mm guns were always present, providing fairly intense and accurate fire. On 8 October Sub-Lieutenant McCartney's aircraft was hit in the engine, forcing him to bale out over the sea. He was safely recovered by destroyer. The Merlin engine was rather vulnerable to damage, although David Lees-Jones managed to fly back about 100 miles with no oil pressure showing. He had been hit in the oil tank but it was thought that the slipstream kept just enough in the tank to keep the engine running. I also had a lucky break. I landed on safely but couldn't move the throttle to taxi across the barrier. It was jammed solid, corroded by salt water! On 10 October our second sortie into the Aegean ended and we returned to Alexandria.

On 15 October we arrived off the coast of Greece to provide top cover for Greek ships landing Allied soldiers in the Athens area. Whilst on patrol in the Senior Pilot's flight I sighted an aircraft 1,000 feet above at nine o'clock to us. David Ogle left John Brittain and me on patrol and he and his Number Two went to investigate. It was a Ju 188 and it was promptly attacked and shot down. On return to patrol our area we were followed by a lone aircraft above and behind us. I was sent to investigate. Seeing that it was a Spitfire, I returned and continued patrolling our sector. The lone Spitfire persisted in following us, always above and behind. I went after it again and flew in close formation with it. The aircraft had no squadron markings, only British roundels and serial number EN290. The pilot sat motionless looking at me and after a few minutes in company I broke away and re-joined the Senior Pilot. On our return to the ship we were unable to trace or identify the aircraft, and I have often wondered whether it was being flown by a German.

Allied troops had little opposition getting ashore, and on 17 October the carrier squadrons returned to interdiction against shipping and rail targets.

It soon became obvious that the Germans were making a final effort to evacuate as many troops as possible, and as we attacked their lines of communication the flak became increasingly intense and our casualties increased. One of *Emperor*'s pilots baled out safely, but one of 807 Squadron's pilots was not so lucky. He inverted his aircraft to bale out, but the Seafire went into a spiral dive and hit the water before he could leave the cockpit. In a Seafire it was always better to step out of the cockpit on to the wing if possible, before pulling the rip-cord. The same day a railway junction at Kavini was attacked and several trains were completely destroyed. In another incident, a Dornier 24 was foolish enough to attempt to take off, and five Seafires pounced on it immediately it became airborne. On 18 October Les Baker's aircraft was hit in the coolant tank. He baled out near Mount Olympus and managed to evade capture and return to the Squadron later.

Above: A short respite at Malta for 809 Squadron, here temporarily on board HMS *Attacker*. The aircraft are now Seafire IIIs: notice the down-turned wing tips and the wing-fold jury struts lying horizontally across the wings. The aircraft nearest the camera has the legend 'Guns loaded' scrawled beneath the cockpit.

The next day was hectic for everyone. Airborne in the Senior Pilot's flight, we dive-bombed a merchant ship and a large ferry carrying German soldiers and vehicles. Both were damaged, but they were being escorted by two flak ships and the fire from the latter was so fierce we were surprised that none of us was hit. We then moved to the road running north-west from Larissa and strafed a column of seventeen lorries, trailers and cars spread out along the highway. We left at least six flamers and an enormous fire with a smoke column about 1,000 feet high. On the way back to the strip we sighted and blew up two trains. This had been a remarkable sortie, but evidently one that was typical of those experienced by Naval squadrons that day.

Tony Wood (later Sir Anthony Russell-Wood, Deputy Controller of the Queen's Household) led an unlucky strafing attack on a heavily armed transport column near Mount Olympus. Graham Moore was hit and baled out nearby, but he evaded capture and returned unhurt. David Lees-Jones was hit but managed to reach the sea, where he baled out safely. Tony and his Number Two arrived back on board, each with several flak holes in wings and engine.

On my last flight of the day I was sent to orbit David Lees-Jones until he was picked up by the destroyer HMS *Troubridge*. I was then vectored to intercept a 'bogey' but as I climbed it dived away at high speed and was never sighted. None of us knew it at the time, but those were the last direct actions in which the Squadron was to be involved in against German forces in World War II. That evening we anchored in the harbour at Khios.

We sailed for Alexandria a few days later and were overjoyed to hear that we would shortly be on the way to Malta, Gibraltar and home to give leave and replenish.

Arriving back in Britain early in November, the Squadron and ship's company enjoyed two weeks of well-earned leave, and on a personal note I was extremely fortunate to be at home with my wife when my son was born on 18 November. We were both most appreciative of an extended period of leave approved by my Squadron Commander and

Captain Leonard Sinker, the Captain of HMS *Stalker*—without any request from me. I have always thought it was a marvellous gesture in time of war. The Navy really does look after its own.

Towards the end of the month we flew new L.III Seafires aboard *Stalker*, and soon afterwards Lieutenant-Commander Norman Lester took over as our Squadron Commander. Early in December the Squadron embarked in HMS *Attacker* for passage to Gibraltar and onwards to Dekheila, Alexandria.

It has been an eventful year. We all felt that we had played an effective part in supporting the Allied armies and in covering miscellaneous operations at sea, but we were very surprised that few of us had seen an enemy aircraft in the air. The Seafire had performed amazingly well in the various tasks and rôles assigned to it, but in low wind conditions we all still needed to give each deck landing the full concentration, care and attention so essential for a safe arrival. It would also have been useful if the aircraft's range and endurance could have been improved.

An important move to the Far East was expected, and we wondered how we would fare there . . .

To the Far East
In late January 1945, 809 Squadron was again firmly based at Dekheila, and the next month was spent with our new Squadron Commander and working up many new faces amongst both aircrew and service personnel.

On 1 March we were reunited with HMS *Stalker* and on the 5th the Squadron gave a bombing and strafing demonstration for King Farouk. In return the king flooded the ship with oranges for the ship's company and Squadron ratings and gave each pilot a gold cigarette lighter. Being a non-smoker, I sent my lighter to my father, who was serving in the RAF. A few weeks later I received a rather bemused reply saying that he appreciated the gift but that the gold seemed to have peeled off You can't win them all!

After a short spell with 809 Squadron, Norman Lester was relieved by Lieutenant-Commander Andrew ('Pants') Bloomer as Commanding Officer, and on about 13 March HMS *Stalker* sailed for the Suez Canal en route to join the East Indies Fleet. We disembarked to Katukurunda (Ceylon) on 20 March and were soon joined by 807 and 879 Squadrons. The three carriers, *Hunter*, *Attacker* and *Stalker*, were reunited using the harbour at Trincomalee as their base. The Japanese carrier fleet was fully occupied in the Pacific Ocean and it was unlikely to pose a threat to the East Indies Fleet. We realised, however, that we would still face a formidable threat from shore-based enemy aircraft and our interdiction and army support rôle would be over jungle terrain.

The Japanese Mitsubishi Zero was a light aircraft without any protective armour plating and could outmanoeuvre a Seafire in a sustained turn. We had tried clipping the wing tips on some of our aircraft, which allowed us to roll into a turn more quickly, but unfortunately it increased the radius in a full turn compared to our unclipped Seafires.

The RAF had obtained a Zero and test pilots had evaluated its performance against the Seafire. This resulted in a specialist RAF team being sent to Ceylon to instruct pilots on the tactics most likely to be effective against Japanese fighters. The team spent a few weeks with our squadrons in Ceylon using Harvards, in which they gave dual instruction to demonstrate recommended tactics. The Seafire could out-climb and out-dive a Zero, and 'dive and zoom' became the basis for future air combat training.

Most of the terrain over which we flew was quite different from that in Europe and North Africa. Main roads were few, and most of the areas being fought over were covered by inhospitable jungle. It was often impossible to see the target at which one was firing as it was hidden by trees. Very close co-operation between pilot and Forward Air Controller was essential as the direction of fire required by the Army was indicated by the FAC using any prominent landmark available—often a hill, an outcrop of rock or a particularly large tree. The distance of the target from the landmark was estimated by the FAC and it was hoped that the pilots' judgement was in unison.

As our own troops would usually be in fairly close contact with the enemy, we were constantly worried about our accuracy and the danger of 'friendly fire'. However, the Army seemed to like our precision and on occasions would call for two or three firing runs followed by non-firing runs to simulate our troops launching an attack—when the enemy had their heads down!

Operations over the jungle also required adequate survival training in the event of being forced down. We all experienced a few days and nights in the jungle of southern Ceylon and learnt the essential basics of successful survival. We didn't see a single snake but detested the leeches that were always present! We also knew that the Japanese were not inclined to be kind to 'downed' pilots, so we flew with a .38 pistol, a Gurkha *kukri* and a Sten machine gun, all of which had to be crammed into the Seafire's small cockpit. Fortunately, none of us was required to 'stand and deliver'.

Early in April the CO and a few of our pilots were temporarily attached to an RAF squadron close to Akyab in Burma in order to gain first-hand

Opposite: HMS *Stalker*, followed by her sister-ship *Attacker*, takes passage through the Suez Canal en route to join the East Indies Fleet, March 1945; HMS *Hunter* led the trio. The Seafire IIIs have freshly applied markings, and their codes now consist of three characters rather than two. A Harvard trainer is parked near the round-down. Right: Once in the Far East, all red paint was removed from the markings of Royal Navy aircraft lest, in the heat of battle, they be mistaken for Japanese. Roundels took on a variety of forms, but the style of that shown here was common. The photograph was taken on board HMS *Stalker*, but the 'prang' evidently involves a Seafire Mk III from a visiting squadron.

Left: A Seafire pilot practises his skills over the forbidding jungle terrain of Ceylon. Survival training was an especially important aspect of the preparation for all aircrew serving with the East Indies Fleet.
Below: A glimpse into HMS *Stalker*'s hangar, spring 1945. As well as having had their national markings altered, the Seafires have now been decorated with broad white bands across their wings, tailplanes and fins, further to aid distant recognition.
Right, upper: Lieutenant Ray Rawbone makes his one hundredth deck landing in a Seafire. HMS *Stalker*, 6 June 1945.
Right, lower: A barrier encounter for an 809 Squadron Seafire III, resulting in a damaged propeller. Notice that the tailwheel has also been sheared off.

experience against the Japanese. Having recently been appointed Senior Pilot, however, I was left behind to continue our work-up. Most of our New Zealand and Australian pilots had left us to return to their homelands, and a number of replacements had arrived. They included four pilot officers who had transferred from the RAF, one of whom was David Morgan, who after the war became one of Vickers' top test pilots. During this period Don Mant baled out and landed safely in a palm tree!

Generally speaking, our operations with the East Indies Fleet were nowhere near as intensive as those in the Mediterranean Sea or as those experienced by Allied carriers in the Pacific theatre. Endless combat patrol over the Fleet became our first priority, and, apart from the CO's detachment to Burma, live ground-attack sorties in support of the Army against Japanese formations were few and far between.

Hunter, *Stalker* and *Attacker* made several incursions into the Bay of Bengal and around the Andaman and Nicobar Islands. In company with HMS *Khedive* and HMS *Ameer*, we also gave cover to the Fleet in support of air strikes against targets in northern Sumatra. During one of these attacks 'Lofty' Tomlinson, who had joined the Navy with me in 1942, was covering the strike aircraft in a Hellcat when he disappeared. For many years I wondered what happened to him but it was not until I retired that I learnt that he had been forced to ditch or bale out over the sea. He was picked up by a fishing vessel and taken to Singapore, where he was handed over to the Japanese. In late July, just before the war ended, he was marched out of prison together with two Royal Marine officers and beheaded. He was just twenty-two.

On 24 April we sailed to cover the invasion of Rangoon. On 2 May we flew low cover over the beaches, and it soon became clear that there was little opposition. Local inhabitants and our ex POWs had posted 'Japs gone' in large letters on the roofs and we did not see a single enemy aircraft. General Slim was obviously well on the way to recapturing the whole of Burma. We carried out armed reconnaissance and a photo-recce of the coast of Malaya before returning to Trincomalee.

Shortly afterwards the Squadron suffered the loss of three pilots. On 31st May Sub-Lieutenant McCartney was killed whilst dive-bombing. His bomb appeared to hit his propeller on release and his aircraft exploded, giving him no chance to escape. Late in July our Wing Leader, George Baldwin, led a twenty-four-aircraft wing formation over

SEAFIRE

Left, upper: Armourers prepare 20mm cannon feed belts for their Seafires at RNAS Katukurunda, Ceylon. The 'D-5' codes on the aircraft identify them as belonging to 807 Squadron.
Left, lower: A trio of 809 Squadron's Seafire IIIs over their carrier, HMS *Stalker*, in the summer of 1945.
Above: Deck-landing accidents continued to be regular occurrences throughout 1945, this 809 Squadron Seafire having had it Merlin engine wrenched from its mountings as a result of one.

north-eastern Ceylon during which Sub-Lieutenants Morrison and Davis collided and baled out over the jungle. After three exhausting days spent searching with native guides they were both found by Squadron search teams but, sadly, they had both been killed on contact with the ground.

In another incident, I had just landed on deck, followed by Don Mant. After switching off in the deck park we were sheltering in the catwalks, after the usual rapid exit from our aircraft, when the third aircraft hit the barrier. The collision triggered both cannon and machine-gun fire, which passed perilously close to our position—so close, in fact, that a cannon or machine-gun round 'split' Don's leather helmet from front to back without touching his head! After baling out over Ceylon, Don began to think that his nine lives were running out, but he was about to endure a third set-back. He approached the ship to land on and missed the arrester wires. He also missed the barrier, and the ship, and, at low speed, the aircraft dived into the sea. There was no sight of Don until he suddenly appeared about half a mile astern in the ship's wake. He had escaped from the cockpit only to find his Mae West snagged in the aircraft's tailplane. Luckily he was a strong swimmer and was able to free himself as the aircraft sank.

* * *

Fortunately for everyone's peace of mind, the end of the war was in sight and 8 August saw the whole fleet in Trincomalee harbour enjoying VJ-Day. Our excitement was short-lived, however, as the general commanding Japanese forces in Malaya stated that he would not surrender and vowed to fight on. Thus we were at sea again on 20 August when I made my first interception of an enemy aircraft. It was a Japanese twin-engine military passenger aircraft code-named 'Tabby'—ironically, a Japanese version of the American DC-3 Dakota that had been licensed for production before the outbreak of the Pacific War. I was immediately ordered not to shoot it down! As I closed in the pilot waggled his wings so violently that I thought they might fall off, and I enjoyed a few minutes in close formation before slowly dropping astern—a manœuvre that, clearly, almost frightened the occupants to death!

September 9 saw our carriers off the coast of Malaya to cover 'D-Day' landings north of Port Dickson. There was no opposition, Japanese aircraft were parked on hardstandings without propellers, and as far as could be seen all Allied military demands had been complied with. A few days later *Hunter*, *Stalker* and *Attacker* followed the cruiser and flagship HMS

SEAFIRE

Royalist into Singapore, the first ships to do so at the end of the war.

The next two days were spent in looking after Allied prisoners-of-war, many of whom had been brutally treated by the Japanese. Preparations were made to take some of them on board and bring them home. Meanwhile we were privileged to witness Lord Mountbatten, General Slim, Admiral Power and Air Marshal Park accepting the surrender of the Japanese generals who had been marched through the streets under escort to face justified humiliation and defeat.

We sailed for home shortly afterwards, arriving in Greenock on 22 October. Fate had not finished with us, however: the Squadron disembarked to Nutts Corner before disbanding and during the final formation fly-past Lieutenant David Lees-Jones and his wingman Sub-Lieutenant Siddall collided and, sadly, both were killed.

Left: Some 'prangs' were particularly damaging, involving not only the landing aircraft but also aircraft in the deck park forward. This is another 809 Squadron accident, although it should not be thought that 809 was especially prone to mishap: every Seafire squadron suffered in the same way.

With Hindsight

In 1944–45 in the Mediterranean and in 1945 in the East Indies Fleet, the Allies enjoyed almost unbroken air superiority. Thus, whilst continuous combat air patrols were flown, the Seafire was rarely face to face with the enemy in its designed rôle. Actual contact with enemy forces was usually made during army-support, ground-attack or interdiction sorties—all essential, but secondary rôles, and rôles for which the aircraft had to be adapted or modified. In its main air combat rôle the Seafire was always superb, but in its secondary duties it lacked range and was not as robust in the face of flak as some American carrier-borne aircraft. Nevertheless, its versatility was effective and potent. After the war I was lucky enough to fly every subsequent mark of Seafire except the Mark 46 with contra-rotating propellers. The Griffon-engine aircraft were more powerful but needed greater care and control because of the more severe torque on take-off. They were faster and more advanced, but in my view none allowed that feeling of *joie de vivre* so apparent in the early marks.

Above: Three 809 Squadron Seafire IIIs fly in close formation. This photograph predates the lower photograph on page 76: although two of the aircraft here have the same codes, all three have their fuselage markings in different positions (the outline of the original, larger roundel can be made out), they retain European-theatre (Type 'C') fin flashes and they lack the broad white identification panels. The aircraft leading is L.III NF434, which appears, nearest the camera, in earlier *décor* on page 74.

SEAFIRE AT WAR—2

Commander Tommy Handley MiD

THE Admiralty arranged for me to fly out to Singapore to join 800 Squadron in the last few days of 1949. The flight proved to be most interesting. The aircraft was a Super Constellation of British Overseas Airways Corporation (later to become British Airways). It was the principal long-haul aircraft of the time, driven by four piston engines, and it carried 66 passengers. On the first day we took off from London and made for our first port of call at Rome, from where, after a two-hour sight-seeing tour, we took off for Cairo. After an overnight stop at the famous and fabulous Shepherds Hotel, one of the most prestigious hotels in the Empire (I remember that, on each floor, there was a tall black Sudanese dressed in a long white robe and turban and carrying a large curved sword; we never found out whether they were there to keep us in our rooms or to keep others out), we had a long-haul flight to Karachi. Here we refuelled and were then taken straight off to Calcutta, although inclement weather required a diversion to Allahabad. It was morning when we landed, and after a couple of hours on the ground the weather had cleared at Calcutta and we were able to fly on there. The next stop was Singapore, in the late evening, and although I was due to leave the flight I was taken with the rest of the passengers for a night's rest at yet another of the Empire's great hotels, Raffles.

Below: Three of 800 Squadron's complement of Seafire 47s form the centrepiece of HMS *Triumph*'s flight deck as the ship is manned during her departure from Grand Harbour, Malta, en route to the Far East, July 1949. The carrier was on station in Japanese waters when the Korean War broke out in June the following year

In those days there was no air conditioning, and we slept under mosquito nets. Next morning I was collected by naval transport and taken to RNAS Sembawang, where I signed in with 800 Naval Air Squadron. It was back to reality!

Sembawang was a small grass airfield which had been built during the war by British prisoners-of-war under the direction of the Japanese occupying forces. Not quite finished when the war ended, it was completed by the British soon afterwards and handed over to the RN. We put down Sommerfeld tracking, long strips of metal plating secured together to form a semblance of a runway. Our accommodation was in Japanese 'Basher' huts, which were made of wood, including a wooden floor, and when my Chinese steward, by the name of Chan Fukoi (pronounced as spelt) and wearing wooden flip-flops came to call me in the morning I could hear his footsteps miles away.

I did not care for my first few trips from Sembawang in a Seafire 47. It was a very hot and humid climate and one never stopped perspiring—and climbing into a very hot metal aircraft that had been standing in sun for a while made matters even worse. The noise of the aircraft wheels on the metal tracking had to be experienced to be believed. When airborne it took a while to become acquainted to flying over thick jungle instead of the rather lovely English fields, villages and countryside. At this time the Communist confrontation was taking place in Malaya and the Army were very much involved. Occasionally they asked us to fire live rockets into a selected grid square in the hope that the bandits would be put to flight and driven into their sights.

Although I had flown most marks of Seafires, including the 15 and 17, both fitted with the bigger Griffon engine, I only had four flights in a Mk 47 in Britain before departing for the Far East. However I was most impressed with it: it was a superb aeroplane in the air and a better fighter than any of the previous marks; it could, moreover, carry a greater weapon load and had a better range and endurance. The Rolls-Royce Griffon fitted with the injector pump was a most reliable powerplant, and the Squadron experienced no engine failures of any kind. The six-bladed contra-rotating propellers were a big advance, and even at full throttle on take-off there was no tendency to swing. There was, furthermore, no change in longitudinal stability during a dive—which helped enormously when we were operating in the ground-attack rôle. It was a great aircraft to fly and fight, and the only trouble was that the fuselage was not up to carrier operations: it was inadequate in the face of the stresses and strains imposed on the aircraft whilst deck landing and catching a wire.

My first few weeks with 800 Squadron were awesome to say the least; perhaps traumatic would be a better word. My Flight consisted of four aircraft, with myself as Leader; however, all three of my pilots were to experience bad accidents within a month of my joining the Squadron. The first involved Lieutenant Bill Heard, who had been one of the half-dozen of our fighter instructors at Henstridge. He was flying as my Number Three and was Deputy Leader of the Flight. During an exercise over the sea just to the north of the Malaysian peninsula he reported that his engine was overheating and that he was returning to base immediately. By the time he had reached Singapore Island his engine was boiling and he elected to land on the first airfield he came to. This was RAF Changi, but unfortunately there was a large four-engined aircraft landing at the same time and so he decided to do a 'wheels up' on the grass alongside the runway. He hit a tree and was killed. My Number Two in 71 Flight, Commissioned Pilot Dick Peters, had been one of my pupils at RAF Syerston in 1948, and in making a deck landing on HMS *Triumph* one day found himself too far over to

Above: HMS *Triumph* at Flying Stations off Japan, June 1950, about to launch a dozen of her Fireflies and Seafires for a practice strike. Each aircraft will make a free take-off, and therefore the longest possible length of flight deck is required. The ship's first launch 'in anger' occurred on 3 July. Below: The 13th Carrier Air Group—i.e., *Triumph*'s complement of 800 Squadron Seafires and 827 Squadron Fireflies—disembarked at Sembawang, Singapore, in February 1950. The Fireflies are F.R. Mk 1s.

the port side. He caught an arrester wire, but ended up standing on his nose in the port walkway. Fortunately, he was able to slide down the nose of the Seafire and escape to fight another day. My Number Four was Lieutenant Lew Stone. During deck landing practice on another carrier he missed the arrester wires and ended up in the steel wire barriers. The aircraft burst into flames, the aircraft was bent at the cockpit and the firemen rescuers had great difficulty in extracting him. They did get him out, but he was badly burned on the lower legs, arms and face. He never flew again and at a later date I met him after he had remustered as a fighter direction officer. I personally witnessed the last two of these accidents as I had landed on immediately before both of them. So I was given two new pilots and three new Seafires and we got on with it. There was no counselling for poor Dick Peters—he was flying the next day! We had to get back to Hong Kong as rapidly as possible, in order to help the Army garrison repel the massive Communist Chinese forces who were pushing south in the direction of the colony. We, together with the one RAF squadron of Spitfires at Kai Tak, would be the entirety of the island's air defence. As the Army had only some 10,000 troops to fight a Chinese Army at least a million strong there would be little hope for any of us. Luckily, Chairman Mao Tse-Tung, it transpired, was interested only in clearing

85

his country of the Nationalists and did not bother about Hong Kong, which was something of a relief.

After a few weeks 800 (Seafire 47) and 827 (Firefly) Squadrons embarked in *Triumph* and we made our way up to Hong Kong: entering the port and suddenly turning the corner to see Victoria Island on the port side and Kowloon in the New Territories on the starboard was a never-to-be-forgotten experience. Before the ship entered harbour both squadrons had flown off a few aircraft to the local airfield at Kai Tak so that aircrew could have flying practice. The ship was based on Hong Kong but would periodically depart in order to conduct exercises. On one occasion the exercise was with the US Fleet, and afterwards we went to their base at Subic Bay in the Philippines, where we were received with great friendship and hospitality from the Americans. In late March we heard we were to go to Japan for three months to be temporarily part of the Allied occupation forces. This was all exciting stuff, but we were a little apprehensive: after all, we had been at war with them less than five years before.

On 15 April 1950 both squadrons took off from *Triumph* in the Inland Sea of Japan at 0630 and flew around in formation waiting for the Royal Australian Air Force station at Iwakuni to open. We had flown off early as the ship wanted to enter Kure at 0800. In the event the Aussies saw us flying around and opened early, and by 0800 all twenty-five of our aircraft had landed and switched off engines in dis-

persal. We were made very welcome by the Royal Australian Air Force and it was wonderful to be ashore at an airfield again and free to fly as and when we needed to as opposed to flying to a strict carrier cycle of turning into wind every one and a half hours or so. Our first introduction to the Japanese was in the Officers' Mess as they carried out the duties of cooks, stewards and batmen. We found them very efficient, hard-working, keen to please and subservient. There was no sign of bitterness or hostility and our initial apprehensiveness was soon dispelled. The airfield itself had been an operational Japanese base during the war and in the latter stages had been used to launch 'Kamikaze' suicide attacks against the British and American fleets.

The airfield was a few miles from the large village of Iwakuni and some fifty miles South of Hiroshima, the town over which the first atomic bomb had been detonated. On driving out of the airfield I was struck by the beauty of the Japanese cherry trees: they were everywhere, and, in full blossom, a wonderful sight. The countryside was scenic and most attractive, there was a river running by the village with an old wooden bridge crossing it. I remember walking over this bridge, which was for pedestrians only, having left my camera on the back seat of our open Jeep and, on our return to the vehicle, finding it still on the back seat. My RAAF guide remarked that the locals were very trustworthy, and stealing other people's property was almost unknown in this countrified part of Japan. Hiroshima was a magnet to us, of course, and we each made our way by train at some time or another to see the devastated city. I remember climbing up the inside of the only building that remained standing, and viewing the scene from the cupola on top, which has become such a famous landmark today.

After six weeks ashore at Iwakuni, during which time *Triumph* had been in dock at Kure, the Squadrons re-embarked and we began a splendid circumnavigation of Japan. We called in at Kobe, Osaka, Yokosuka (a naval base some forty miles south of Tokyo, and full of the US Navy) and Ominato. Whilst at Kobe we paid a visit to Kyoto, the ancient capital of Japan, and walked round the Old Imperial Palace with its Shinto shrines, beautiful gardens and small lakes with interconnecting wooden bridges. In Yokosuka we worked tropical routine, and some of us took a few days' leave, which was spent in Tokyo. The city was in a poverty-stricken state. They had no finances to cope with repairs and re-decoration— little, in fact, had been done since the war—and there were few motor cars on the roads, which themselves were in a terrible state of repair.

Our last port of call was to Ominato, on Hokkaido, the northernmost island. This was the 'Japanese Scapa Flow', whence the Imperial Fleet had set out to make the infamous attack on Pearl Harbor. It was remote and, as far as I can remember, uninhabited. I don't really know why we went there, but possibly the thought was that the Allies might use it against a new enemy. Russia perhaps? China maybe? Luckily it was only for a couple of days, and during this time I went ashore with other aviators to inspect the disused airfield, now very overgrown and quite unusable. Back on board there was a great

Left: Rocket-Assisted Take-Off Gear (RATOG), unchanged in configuration and operation from that employed during the World War II years (see page 14), was available to 800 Squadron's Seafire pilots, offering the advantage of a shortened take-off run for a fully loaded aircraft. In the upper photograph, the aircraft is abreast the island on its run and the gear is on the point of being activated; in the lower picture, the RATOG has been fired, accompanied by the inevitable clouds of smoke.
Right: Commissioned Pilot 'Bunny' Warren (left) and Lieutenant (now Admiral Sir) John Treacher discuss tactics during a break in Seafire operations on board HMS *Triumph*.

SEAFIRE

Left: One of 800 Squadron's Seafire 47s on finals, HMS *Triumph*, 1950. The edge of the batsman's screen can be seen at far right.

Left: A Seafire is hauled to a stop by *Triumph*'s No 2 wire; notice the raised safety barrier amidships, a 'second line of defence' protecting the aircraft parked forward in case of accident. The aircraft's markings are unusual, to say the least: the starboard wing has a modern, Type 'D' roundel, the port wing a World War II Type 'B' and the fuselage a mid-1940s Type 'C1'. The fin code and fuselage call-sign are painted in a very pale colour.

Left: Another arrest by No 2 wire, this time of a more conventionally marked aircraft. On the flight deck at right can be seen one of the bow springs that kept the arresting cable some four inches above the deck when aircraft were landing on; this was retracted to lie on the deck surface at all times other than when recovery was taking place.

Right: A hit is scored on a small coaster off western Korea, September 1950. During the summer of that year, 13th CAG aircraft began to be painted up with black and white identification stripes around the wings and fuselage, reminiscent of the 'D-Day' invasion markings applied to Allied aircraft in the summer of 1944.

atmosphere. Our foreign meanderings were over and we were starting on our way back home, and to the family.

Or so we thought . . .

* * *

We were off Kyushu, the most southerly of the Japanese main islands, when we heard on the BBC World Service that war had broken out between North and South Korea, just a couple of hundred miles way over on our starboard side. As we had a drink in the Wardroom bar that night we all agreed this was the one war in which we—the British Empire, the Royal Navy and certainly HMS *Triumph* —would not be involved. So we had a second gin, a good supper, and a good night's rest. Everything looked rosy. At breakfast next morning, however, we heard that we were no longer bound for Hong Kong. During the night, after instructions from the Admiralty, the ship had altered course to head for Okinawa. It appeared that we were going to be involved after all. Could we be forgiven that a little despondency set in?

We were about to become involved in what appeared to us to be a civil war: we would be on the side of those in the south who faced north against those in the north who wanted to move south! The British government had decided to go along with United Nations Security Council Resolution 82 and we were going to be at war again. Our orders were to proceed to Okinawa, some 400 miles south of the tip of Japan, and the island that had been the scene of some bitter fighting between the Americans and the Japanese immediately before the atom bombs were dropped. We were to join up with the US Navy aircraft carrier *Valley Forge* and await instructions. In late June and after one sail ashore in one of the ship's whalers, and a variety show on board provided by the American equivalent of our wartime ENSA, *Valley Forge* and *Triumph* set sail for the west coast of Korea. Just before arriving we separated, having been given our respective targets, and we prepared for our attack on Kaishu airfield.

Kaishu was on the coast, on the western side of the front line between the opposing forces. The targets were to be aircraft on the ground, the hangars and control tower. Twenty-four RN aircraft took part in the raid—twelve Fireflies and twelve Seafires. The Seafires were to be the covering force and to defend the Fireflies in case of enemy fighter attack, but we were carrying six 60-pound rocket projectiles each so could have a go at the airfield should no enemy air opposition be encountered. None was forthcoming, and as we neared the target there were no aircraft on the ground either, so we all carried out attacks on the hangars, workshops and control tower. An air of mystery prevailed. Where was the enemy? In the recce photos taken by the Americans a few days earlier there had been plenty of aircraft on the airfield. They had probably all been flown elsewhere along the front line.

For the next week or so my flying logbook shows that I was employed on combat air patrol whilst the Fireflies carried out sea patrols. The Americans employed us in a defensive rôle for the fleet, as at this stage it was uncertain whether the Chinese or even the Russians were going to join forces with the North Koreans. As no enemy appeared on the sea or in the air it was decided that *Triumph*'s aircraft would attack any waterborne targets that could be found, and also undertake a few special missions. During the next ten weeks I flew some 35 sorties, involving a rocket attack on landing craft in Chinnampo; a strafing attack with 20mm cannon on MTBs and gunboats in Wonsan harbour; spotting for the guns of the destroyer HMS *Cossack* bombarding Mockpo, and spotting for the cruiser HMS *Kenya* bombarding Inchon (both carried out in Neptune aircraft of, and flown by, the US Navy); a strike on oil tanks at Mockpo; bombardment spotting for the cruiser HMS *Jamaica* at Kunsan railway yards (this time in one of our own Seafires); many armed recces of the sea lanes and harbours of North and South Korea (during which we blew the front end off a coaster and sank several armed junks); several photo recces of ports and harbours (including Chinnampo, which was particularly unfriendly and usually gave us plenty of anti-aircraft fire); and finally, in company with my Senior Pilot (Lieutenant 'Sheepy' Lamb), an armed recce of Chinnampo and the ports and harbours of

Above: 800 Squadron's Seafire Mk 47 VP495/'181-P' abandons a landing on board HMS *Triumph*— too high—and prepares to go round again for a second attempt. The black and white stripes, confined to the wings, have obliterated the national markings and the letters of the serial number.
Left: The Ops Room on board HMS *Triumph* in 1950: (left to right) Captain A. D. Torlesse DSO, Rear-Admiral W. G. Andrewes (Flag Officer Second-in-Command Far East Fleet), Lieutenant-Commander George Creese (Commander Ops) and Commander Merlin Bruce (Commander Air).
Right: 800 Squadron Seafire pilots arrive at Iwakuni from on board *Triumph*: (left to right) Lieutenants Tommy Handley, Ian Berry and John Treacher.

the west coast of North Korea to within fifty miles of the Chinese border. One of the targets we found was a water pumping station, and we left it in a pretty parlous state. Quite amazingly during this sortie, we never saw an enemy aircraft or ship, and yet we had ventured some 200 miles into North Korean territory and not far from the border with Communist China.

During our time in Korea we used Sasebo in southern Japan for rest and recreation, and here we had the first-class facilities of the US Navy, including their Officers' Club. It was in the American sector and the Yanks, God bless 'em, had their feet well and truly under the table! A lot of them had taken up with the local populace, and I once saw an enlisted soldier with a young Japanese lady on each arm. Such virility!

When we entered the Korean War the front line ran approximately through the middle of the peninsula. In the early weeks the Allies were pushed down to the south-eastern edge, and then General MacArthur, once his reinforcements arrived, took the initiative and the Allies ended up in North Korea, not far from the Chinese border. We thought it was all over, and *Triumph* was released from the conflict. Our successor on station, HMS *Theseus*, which had Sea Furies rather than Seafires embarked, waited for us in Hong Kong to conduct a turnover. Our spirits were on the crest of the wave and we told them that they had 'missed the boat' and that we had had all the glory. Little did we realise at the time that things were to go wrong for us. The Chinese gave their backing to the North, MacArthur asked permission to use nuclear weapons and was refused, and there was a retreat back to the original front line. *Theseus* was called to the action and endured a real conflict.

Half way through our Korean War episode, on 29 August 1950, we had a most unfortunate accident. The Commanding Officer of 800 Squadron was watching a recovery of aircraft through the Operations Room scuttle when one of 827's Fireflies came in to land with the hook not down. The aircraft entered the wire barriers, the wooden airscrew came off and one blade flew straight at the scuttle. Lieutenant-Commander Ian MacLachlan was hit in the face and died within thirty minutes—a very tragic and completely unexpected turn of events. I was immediately informed that I was now taking over

Above and below: A spectacular 'prang' on board HMS *Triumph* in July 1949, while the ship was on passage to the Far East. VR965, coming in to land, missed the wires and nose-dived into the safety barrier, resulting in a semi-detached forward fuselage. These two photographs depict the aftermath, with the aircraft's recovery under way. Notice the scorched and foam-strewn surfaces of the flight deck. The pilot, mercifully, was unhurt. Opposite page: October 1950: her task off Korea completed, HMS *Triumph* returns home and is seen here off Aden. Within weeks the Seafire would pass from service as a Royal Navy front-line fighter, its duties now transferred to the Hawker Sea Fury.

command of the Squadron. This was confirmed by a signal from Admiralty, and I was made up to Acting Lieutenant-Commander.

I had been sent out to *Triumph* and the 13th Carrier Air Group not only as Senior Pilot of the Seafire squadron but also as the Air Group Air Weapons Officer. On the AWO course we had been taught air strategy and tactics and, amongst other things, force requirements to achieve a certain measure of success, for example, the destruction of an enemy's oil industry and the annihilation of a country's electricity grid. I did give a few lectures about air tactics to the Air Group's aircrew, but, as can be imagined, I felt I had been a little over-trained when only once was I called for to give my opinion as to whether the Fireflies should use rockets or bombs to destroy a relatively small rail bridge!

On the way home we called at Singapore, where we were interviewed about our exploits in the Korean War, by the local broadcasting station. Then it was on to Aden and through the Suez Canal, which meant, as the Canal was administered by the British in those days, that we were given a priority passage. I remember we passed a large P&O passenger ship bound for the Far East that had been moored to one side to enable *Triumph* to pass unheeded. All the passengers were on deck to give us a great cheer. We sailed on to Malta, and finally Portsmouth, where we hove to alongside South Railway Jetty, the prime berth, where the BBC came on board to televise an interview for the news later that evening. I was greeted by my wife Elizabeth on the jetty—and what a wonderful meeting it was after eleven months away. Later my parents, who had brought Elizabeth down for the ship's homecoming, arrived.

The Korean War was the Seafire/Spitfire's swan-song; we had flown the last operational missions in this very famous aircraft. Readers will have seen, or at least heard of, the wartime film *First of the Few*, inspired by Prime Minister Winston Churchill's famous words about 'The Few'; we must surely be considered the 'Last of the Few'! However, although the Spitfire was a fine aircraft in the air, it was sadly lacking in deck-landing capability. It had been built to have a high top speed and performance and for operation from shore airfields and it was not robust enough to withstand the stresses and strains of deck operation. The aircraft's skin between the cockpit and the tailplane used to wrinkle if a deck landing was heavy or off the carrier's centre line; indeed, during the Korean War the ship's Air Engineer Officer, in the interests of keeping the aircraft flying, would routinely turn a blind eye to the regulations and the acceptable limits for safety that had been laid down. As soon as the last operational sortie had been flown, however, he grounded every Seafire on board. Thus we were unable to fly during the passage home even if we had wanted to. So we read books—I, *inter alia*, *The Forsythe Saga* and thoroughly enjoyed it!

FRONT-LINE SEAFIRE SQUADRONS

Captain Eric Brown CBE DSC AFC

IN the three and a half years that had elapsed between the Navy taking on charge the first of its folding-wing Seafire Mk IIIs late in 1943 and the delivery of the first of its Mk 47s early in 1947, the navalised Spitfire had covered a great deal of water, both from carriers and from shore bases. Seafires had played an important rôle in the air operations immediately preceding and during the Normandy invasion of June 1944 as part of the 2nd Tactical Air Force, flying from bases on the English south coast. At this time, the only Seafire-armed carrier with the Home Fleet was *Furious* (801 and 880 Squadrons), which had been engaged in a series of Norwegian coastal strikes, but it had been joined by *Indefatigable* (887 and 894) in Norwegian strikes and fighter sweeps by the beginning of August, in which month four escort carriers with Seafires—*Attacker* (879 Squadron), *Khedive* (899), *Hunter* (807) and *Stalker* (809)—had played a major part in Operation 'Dragoon', the invasion of the South of France, these vessels and their Seafires subsequently operating in the Aegean.

As previously mentioned, the escort carrier *Atheling* operating in the Indian Ocean had been the first to receive the folding-wing Seafire Mk III when 889 Squadron embarked in May 1944, although this unit was to be disbanded three months later, when, there no longer being a requirement for a fighter escort carrier in the Indian Ocean, *Atheling* proved too slow to serve with the main fleet. There had followed a hiatus of more than three months before Seafires had again joined the Eastern Fleet, *Indefatigable* arriving at Trincomalee in November, still with 887 and 894 Squadrons on board.

The strict range limitations of the Seafire Mk III now began to make themselves increasingly felt; the availability of aircraft such as the Avenger with greatly enhanced operational radii had resulted in a major change in offensive doctrine and the distances now covered by carrier-launched strikes were extended accordingly. The range being called for was well beyond the capability of the Seafire, which, perforce, was restricted to fleet defence, but this was a rôle in which its excellent acceleration and fast climb placed it second to none, and it remained its primary mission after *Indefatigable* commenced operations in the Far East at the beginning of 1945.

The escort carriers *Hunter* and *Stalker*, with 807 and 809 Squadrons, respectively, joined the East Indies Fleet in April 1945 to participate in the following month's Operation 'Dracula', the assault on Rangoon. These carriers were later joined by *Attacker* with 879 Squadron. Meanwhile 887 and 894 Squadrons flew in support of the Okinawa invasion from *Indefatigable*, and in June 801 and 880 Squadrons from *Implacable* were in action at Truk, these two carriers with their four Seafire squadrons mounting strikes on the Japanese home islands with the US Third Fleet during July and August.

With the end of the war in the Pacific and the reduction in the strength of the Royal Navy's air component in consequence, the number of Seafire squadrons diminished rapidly, but this fighter's career was far from over. The last Seafire Mk III-equipped first-line squadron, 801, disbanded in June 1946 with the return from the Far East of *Implacable*, but the newer generation of Griffon-engined Seafires that had just been entering service as the conflict came to an end was to equip the postwar nucleus, which, by August 1946, comprised only four first-line fighter squadrons, 802, 805, 806 and 807, all but the last-mentioned being equipped with the Seafire Mk XV, No 807 having the Mk XVII.

The Mk XV squadrons were deployed aboard *Venerable* (802), *Ocean* (805) and *Glory* (806) during the course of 1946, while the Mk XVIIs of 807 Squadron, which was not allocated to a Carrier Air Group, were deployed for some three months from November 1946 to Lübeck, Germany, where the unit was attached to the 2nd TAF. 802 and 805 Squadrons were disbanded in the following year. Two other squadrons, however, had meanwhile re-formed on Seafires, 800 with Mk XVIIs and 804 with Mk XVs, these embarking on *Triumph* and *Theseus*, respectively, in February 1947. Although re-formed once more, in April 1947, with Seafire Mk XVIIs for service aboard *Ocean*, 805 Squadron was subsequently transferred to the Royal Australian Navy and re-equipped with Sea Furies in August 1948. In the same month, 807 also converted to the Sea Fury and the Navy was left with only two first-line Seafire squadrons, 800 on board *Triumph* and 804 on board *Ocean*, both converting to Mk 47s in February 1948 and April 1949, respectively.

Left: HMS *Implacable*, off Tokyo Bay in September; the Seafire squadrons on board are 801 and 880, and the aircraft are Mk IIIs. Avenger torpedo-bombers of 828 Squadron are seen aft. Also on board *Implacable* at this time, though not apparent in the photograph, were the Fireflies of the soon-to-be-disbanded 1771 Squadron. These four units had made up the 8th CAG (CO Major P. P. Nelson-Gracie RM) in a short-lived system of combining the squadrons of a single carrier into Carrier Air Groups à la US Navy practice.

800 Squadron was to gain the distinction of being the only unit to take the Seafire Mk 47 into action. A month after *Triumph* arrived in Singapore, in September 1949, 800 mounted a number of rocket attacks against Communist terrorist hide-outs from RNAS Sembawang, and when, in the following June, hostilities broke out in Korea, *Triumph* soon arrived off the west Korean coast, 800 making its first rocket attack—the target being the airfield at Haeju—on 4 July 1950. The Seafires continued their participation in the Korean conflict until *Triumph* was finally withdrawn to Hong Kong on 25 September, by which time just one fully serviceable Seafire remained. When the carrier arrived back home two months later, 800 Squadron was disbanded and the Seafire finally passed from first-line Royal Navy service. Of course, it was to linger on with reserve and training units until, as recounted earlier, the last training squadron to operate this type, 764, was disbanded at RNAS Yeovilton on 23 November 1954.

The Seafire had seen more than eight years of first-line service and the number of combat sorties that it flew in that time must surely have approached five figures. For my own part, I regretted its passing as it marked the end of an era. Nobody would pretend that the Seafire had been the ideal carrier fighter, but I had deck-landed it probably more than any other pilot and had never felt anything but exhilaration at the challenge that it presented. It was an aeroplane which seemed tailor-made for the pilot, and I cannot imagine any other aircraft that would have permitted the liberty of the crab-type approach that I and many others used for deck-landing. True, it left much to be desired with regard to robustness, particularly in its early versions, but then it was doing something that it was never meant to do in the first place. It is also true that it was a lousy ditcher, and I witnessed a number of fatal accidents resulting from its emulation of the diving characteristics of a submarine, but it had been designed for fighting not ditching. There were undoubtedly plusses and minuses, but the Fleet Air Arm owes the Seafire an enormous debt of gratitude because it gave the Royal Navy's intake of young wartime fighter pilots the experience of flying the best that there was—an incalculable morale-booster at a critical moment in World War II.

SEAFIRE

800 NAVAL AIR SQUADRON

Located at RNAS Lee-on-Solent, Eglinton, Hal Far, Sembawang *et alibi* and on board HMS *Triumph*.

Commission: 15/08/46–10/11/50 (Seafire Mk XVs 15/08/46–00/02/47, Mk XVIIs 00/01/47–00/04/49, Mk 47s 00/04/49–00/11/50)
Commanding Officers: Lt-Cdr D. G. Parker DSO DSC, Lt-Cdr M. Hordern DSC (12/02/48), Lt-Cdr J. F. Rankin DSC (01/03/46), Lt-Cdr R. Pridham-Wippell RNVR (14/05/48), Lt-Cdr I. M. McLachlan (24/11/49), Lt-Cdr T. D. Handley (29/08/50)
Senior Pilots: Lt T. D. Handley (1949–28/08/50)

Above: Following its postwar recommissioning in August 1946, 800 Squadron flew Seafire Mk XVs for a few months before embarking on board HMS *Triumph* (code letter 'P') for service with the Mediterranean Fleet, by which time it had re-equipped with Mk XVIIs as shown here. The aircraft are ranged for take-off with propellers turning, with 827 Squadron Fireflies ready aft. The upper surfaces of all the aircraft visible here are finished in the standard FAA disruptive camouflage of the day, which comprised Extra Dark Sea Grey and Dark Slate Grey, and the Seafires are fitted with long-range ventral tanks.

Right: 800 Squadron Seafire Mk 47s on board *Triumph* in Grand Harbour, Valletta, with two 'Town' class cruisers in the background. Two of the aircraft have their side numbers repeated along the leading edges of their wings. The photograph was taken in July 1949, probably at about the same time as that on pages 82–83.

96

FRONT-LINE SEAFIRE SQUADRONS

Above: Some of the personnel of 800 Squadron in company with sailors from the US aircraft carrier *Boxer* pose for the camera in front of a Seafire 47 on board HMS *Triumph* off the Philippines in March 1950. The Squadron had already blooded the Mk 47 in combat: five months earlier it had seen action launching rocket strikes against Communists in Negri Sembilan, Malaya. A few months later it would become embroiled in a much more widespread conflict–Korea.

801 NAVAL AIR SQUADRON

Located at RNAS Stretton, Machrihanish, Hatston, Skeabrae *et alibi* and on board HM Ships *Furious* and *Implacable*.

Commission: 07/09/42–03/06/46 (Spitfire Mk VAs/VBs/VBs Hooked 07/09/42–00/10/42, Seafire Mk IBs 00/09/42–00/06/44, Mk IICs 00/10/42–00/06/44, Mk IIIs 00/05/44–00/11/45, Mk XVs 00/09/45–00/06/46)
Commanding Officers: Lt-Cdr F. R. A. Turnbull DSC, Lt-Cdr R. M. Hall (10/09/42), Lt-Cdr H. F. Bromwich (03/11/43), Lt-Cdr S. Jewers RNVR (18/07/44), Lt-Cdr R. M. Crosley DSC* RNVR (01/09/45), Lt-Cdr J. R. Routley RNVR (07/01/46)
Senior Pilots: Not known

Below, left: The stowage of early Seafires on board the modern armoured carriers was seriously handicapped because the aircraft did not incorporate wing folding, which as well as limiting the numbers that could be taken to sea also posed problems when maintenance work was required. HMS *Furious*, however, by virtue of its old-fashioned cruciform lifts, could readily strike them below, as shown in this photograph of 801 Squadron's Seafire Mk IB MB366/'K'.
Below, right: Seafire IB 'X' of 801 Squadron, clearing HMS *Furious*'s stowed windbreak, takes to the air. 801 was the second FAA squadron to receive Seafires, following 807.

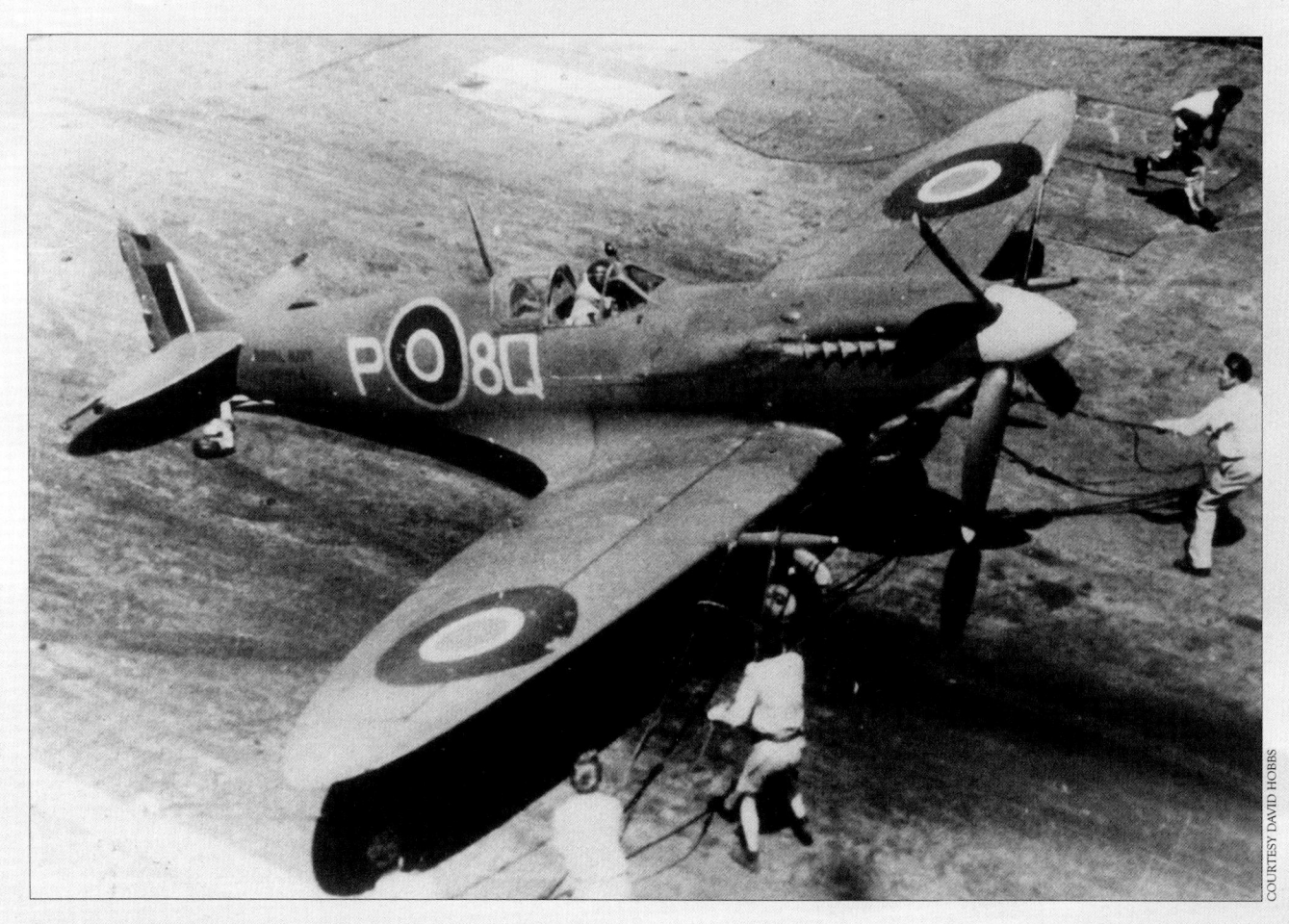

Above: PP934 (it is believed), a Seafire Mk III assigned to 801 Squadron, is freed from the safety barrier on board HMS *Implacable*, at about the time of the carrier's participation in the attacks on the German battleship *Tirpitz* in October 1944. It may be seen that the aircraft's tailwheel has collapsed.
Below: Six months later *Implacable* was in the Far East, en route to fight in the Pacific War: she is seen here, with Seafire IIIs of 801 and 880 Squadrons on board, leaving Sydney, en route to attack the Japanese-held island of Truk. The aircraft are now all wearing the special national markings adopted for the theatre (eliminating the red centre spot, in order to avoid confusion with Japanese aircraft) and carrying long-range tanks.

FRONT-LINE SEAFIRE SQUADRONS

802 NAVAL AIR SQUADRON

Located at RNAS Arbroath, Abbotsinch, Ayr, Yeovilton, Trincomalee, Sembawang, Lee-on-Solent *et alibi* and on board HMS *Venerable*.

Commission: 01/05/45–10/12/52 (Seafire Mk IIIs 01/05/45–00/08/45, Mk XVs 00/08/45–00/04/48)
Commanding Officers: Lt-Cdr R. E. Hargreaves DSC, Lt-Cdr B. H. Harriss (05/01/46), Lt-Cdr M. Hordern DSC (18/05/47)
Senior Pilots: Not known

Left: 802 Squadron's Seafire Mk XV PR348 is drawn to a halt on board HMS *Vengeance*. This is one of the first Mk XVs to have been built, and features the original A-frame arrester hook, an inheritance from the type's Mk III ancestry; later-production Mk XVs were equipped with the 'sting' tail hook at the base of the rudder. It is believed that 802 was the first FAA unit to field a full complement of aircraft wearing the new postwar colour scheme.

803 NAVAL AIR SQUADRON

Located at RNAS Arbroath, Nutts Corner and Lee-on-Solent and NAS Dartmouth, and on board HMCS *Warrior*.

Commission: 15/06/45–01/05/51 (Seafire Mk IIIs 15/06/45–00/12/45, Mk XVs 00/08/45–00/07/47)
Commanding Officers: Lt-Cdr L. D. Wilkinson DSC RNVR, Lt-Cdr A. J. Tanner RCNVR (16/11/45), Lt-Cdr C. G. Watson RCN (00/05/46), Lt-Cdr H. J. G. Bird RCN (05/07/47)
Senior Pilots: Not known

Above and left: PR434 (above) and PR461, both Seafire Mk XVs, in 1947 and with the squadron crest beneath the cockpit proclaiming their affiliation to 803 Squadron, recently transferred to the custody of the Royal Canadian Navy. PR461 has its individual code letter stylised with a light 'shadow'. The two types of arrester hook fitted to Mk XVs may be compared in these two photographs.

99

SEAFIRE

804 NAVAL AIR SQUADRON

Located at RNAS Eglinton, Donibristle, Maydown, Ford *et alibi* and on board HM Ships *Theseus* and *Ocean*.

Commission: 01/10/46–17/11/55 (Seafire Mk XVs 01/10/46–00/03/48, Mk 47s 00/01/48–00/08/49)
Commanding Officers: Lt-Cdr R. F. Bryant, Lt-Cdr S. F. Shotton DSC (11/06/47), Lt-Cdr C. F. Hargreaves (06/02/49)
Senior Pilots: Not known

Left: Only two front-line squadrons would fly the Seafire Mk 47: 800 was one and 804 the other. VP431 of the latter unit is shown, riding the lift on board HMS *Ocean* in 1948. The upper-wing fairings to accommodate the retracted main wheels (inboard) and the four 20mm cannon magazines show up clearly in this photograph.

Right: A new colour scheme and a new carrier—temporarily: 804 Squadron flew their Seafire 47s to HMS *Triumph* for a few days in January 1949 while in the Mediterranean, and one of them, VP445/ '138-0', is seen here, amongst that carrier's Fireflies of 827 Squadron. Clearly the centre of attention, the aircraft appears to have a purpose-made cover shrouding its engine compartment and propeller, with further protection offered to the inboard wing leading edges.

FRONT-LINE SEAFIRE SQUADRONS

Main image: Before receiving MK XVs, 803 Squadron briefly flew Mk IIIs, including this one, NN574. The Squadron was due to take these aircraft out to the Far East, but VJ-Day came and the deployment was cancelled.

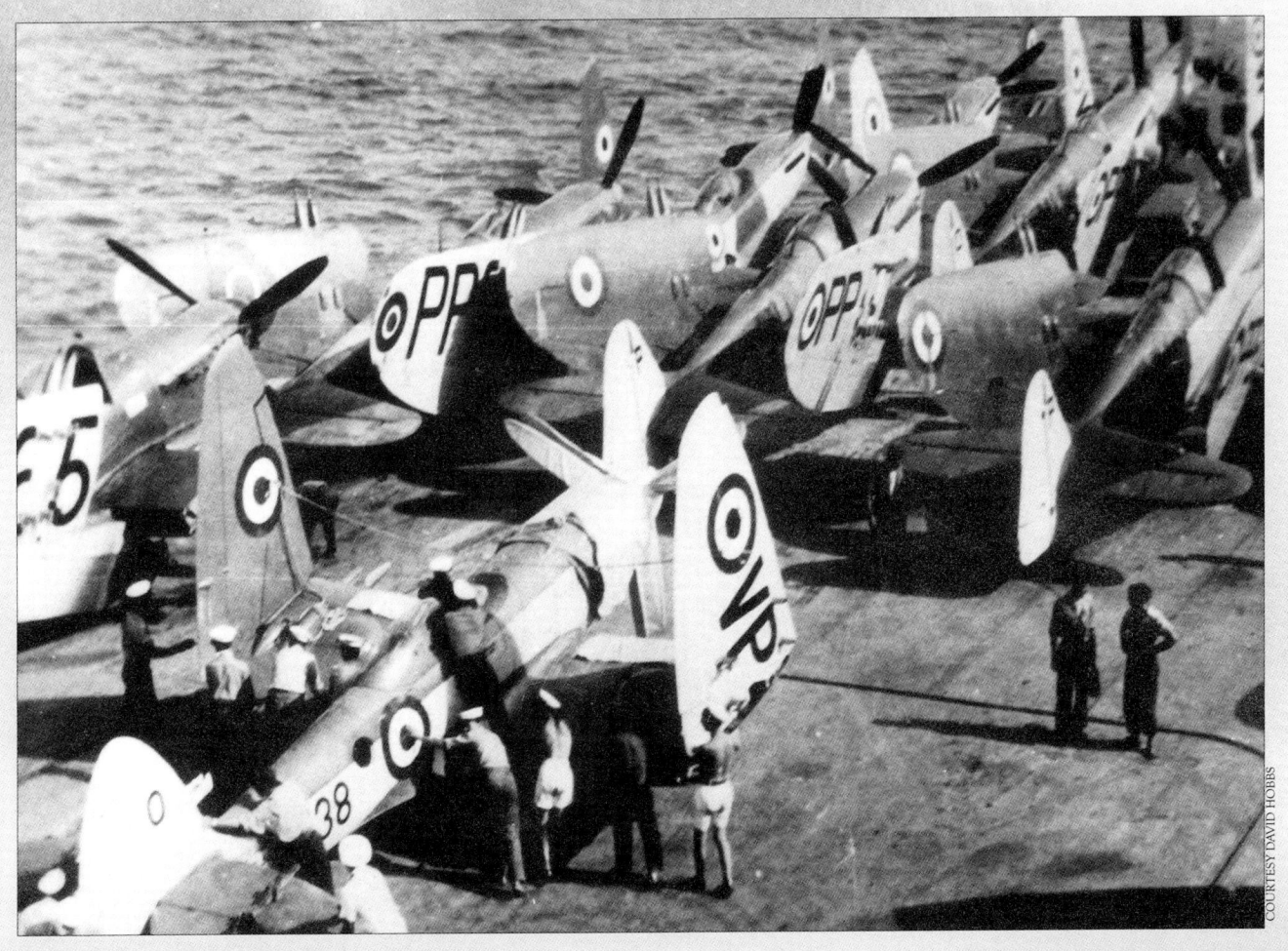

805 NAVAL AIR SQUADRON

Located at RNAS Machrihanish, Lee-on-Solent and Hal Far and on board HMS *Ocean*.

Commission: 01/07/45–01/07/48 (Seafire Mk IIIs 01/07/45–00/08/45, Mk XVs 00/08/45–00/08/46), Mk XVIIs 00/04/47–01/07/48)
Commanding Officers: Lt-Cdr P. J. Hutton DSC RNVR, Lt-Cdr P. E. I. Bailey (28/09/47)
Senior Pilots: Not known

Right: A detail from a larger photograph showing an 805 NAS Seafire XV at Hal Far, Malta, in mid-1946. The aircraft is the personal carriage of CO Lieutenant-Commander Hutton, all of whose aircraft bore the side letter 'J'. The paint finish is the standard disruptive camouflage scheme but with white spinner, code letters, ailerons and wing tips.

Below: Personnel of the 20th Carrier Air Group in August 1947, which comprised 805 Squadron (now Seafire XVIIs) and 812 Firefly F.R.1s and N.F.1s. A Firefly takes centre stage as the principal backdrop here, and unfortunately (for the purposes of this book, at least) Seafires are only partially glimpsed at the flanks.

806 NAVAL AIR SQUADRON

Located at RNAS Machrihanish, Yeovilton, Trincomalee, Kai Tak and Sembawang and on board HMS *Glory*.

Commission: 01/08/45–06/10/47 (Seafire Mk IIIs 01/08/45–00/09/45, Mk XVs 00/09/45–06/10/47)
Commanding Officers: Lt-Cdr A. C. Lindsey DSC, Lt-Cdr A. W. Bloomer (01/01/46), Lt-Cdr R. P. Thurston (01/10/46), Lt-Cdr W. N. Waller (01/06/47)
Senior Pilots: Not known

Left: A rather distant view of Seafire Mk XV SW786, while serving in the Far East in October 1946. The aircraft is wearing Pacific Theatre national markings, even though the war drew to a close over a year previously. At this time, when embarked, the Squadron was serving on board HMS *Glory*, whose deck recognition letter 'Y'—also worn by each of her assigned aircraft, of course—would shortly be changed to 'R'.

FRONT-LINE SEAFIRE SQUADRONS

807 NAVAL AIR SQUADRON

Located at RAF North Front and RNAS Yeovilton, Machrihanish, Hatston, Turnhouse, Colombo Racecourse, Eglinton, Lee-on-Solent *et alibi* and on board HM Ships *Furious*, *Battler*, *Hunter* and *Vengeance*.

Commission: 15/09/40–04/11/55 (Seafire Mk IBs 00/06/42–00/09/42, Mk IICs 00/06/42–00/10/44, Mk IIIs 00/06/44–00/12/45 and 00/09/46–00/10/46, Mk XVIIs 00/12/45–00/09/47)
Commanding Officers: Lt A. B. Fraser-Harris DSC, Lt-Cdr K. Firth RNVR (01/03/43), Lt-Cdr G. C. Baldwin DSC (25/10/43), Lt-Cdr L. G. C. Reece RNZVR (02/06/44), Lt-Cdr E. J. Clark RNVR (10/11/44), Lt-Cdr S. J. Hall DSC (15/03/46), Lt-Cdr R. J. Clark (27/08/46), Lt-Cdr F. R. A. Turnbull DSC* (20/09/46), Lt-Cdr S. J. Hall DSC (02/02/47)
Senior Pilots: Not known

Above, below and right: Pictures of 'prangs' involving Seafires of 807 Squadron while serving on board HMS *Hunter* seem particularly plentiful, and here are three of them. NM995 is seen above and LR752 at right, while the photograph below of aircraft '6-A' is remarkable in that the pilot—'Bob', according to a note on the print—can be seen supporting himself with his arms as he attempts to scramble clear. Gratifyingly, he succeeded!

103

Above: A detachment of Seafire IIIs of 807 Squadron disembarked at Trincomalee, Ceylon, in early summer 1945, the war for this unit to all intents and purposes over as no further combat sorties would be flown.

Below: A nose-over for Seafire III PP979 on board HMS *Hunter*, the *dénouement* of a crash-landing that resulted in a seriously damaged undercarriage. The pilot is unstrapping himself in the cockpit.

808 NAVAL AIR SQUADRON

Located at RNAS St Merryn, Machrihanish, Yeovilton, Burscough, Lee-on-Solent, Henstridge *et alibi* and on board HM Ships *Battler* and *Hunter*.

Commission: 01/01/42–05/12/45 (Spitfire Mk VAs/VBs/VBs Hooked 00/12/42–00/04/43 and 00/02/44–00/07/44, Seafire Mk IICs 00/12/42–00/05/44, Spitfire Mk XIIIs (sic) 00/03/44–00/03/44, Seafire Mk IIIs 00/06/44–00/10/44)
Commanding Officers: Lt C. P. Campbell-Horsfall, Lt-Cdr A. C. Wallace RNVR (17/03/43), Lt-Cdr J. F. Rankin DSC (25/10/43)
Senior Pilots: Not known

Left: A Seafire Mk IIC believed to be from 808 Squadron overruns the flight deck during the unit's work-up on board HMS *Battler* in spring 1943. The Squadron's use of RAF Spitfires in the spring of 1944 occurred during its attachment to the Second Tactical Air Force, when it participated in training exercises for the forthcoming Normandy invasion.

809 NAVAL AIR SQUADRON

Located at RNAS Stretton, Machrihanish and Dale, RAF Long Kesh and North Front and RNAS Dekheila, Katukurunda, Trincomalee and Nutts Corner *et alibi* and on board HM Ships *Unicorn*, *Attacker* and *Stalker*.

Commission: 15/01/41–11/01/46 (Spitfire Mk VAs 00/03/43–00/06/43, Seafire Mk IBs 00/04/43–00/08/43, Mk IICs 00/03/43–00/10/44, Mk IIIs 00/07/44–00/12/45, Mk XVs 00/11/45–00/12/45, Mk XVIIs 00/11/45–00/01/46)
Commanding Officers: Capt R. C. Hay DSC RM, Maj. A. J. Wright RM (01/06/43), Lt-Cdr H. D. B. Eaden RNVR (20/04/44), Lt-Cdr N. H. Lester RNVR (10/11/44), Lt-Cdr A. W. Bloomer (00/03/45)
Senior Pilots: Lt D. Ogle (in 1945), Lt Mason (?) (in 1945), Lt A. R. Rawbone (00/04/45)

Left: A serious landing mishap involving a Seafire Mk IIC of 809 Squadron on board HMS *Stalker* in the Mediterranean. The aircraft appears to have collided with the safety barrier. Spitfires (hence Seafires) were not designed to land on flight decks: their relatively high approach speed and narrow-track main undercarriage may have been acceptable when the aircraft were touching down on dry land, but they were undesirable handicaps when pilots attempted the same thing on narrow sea-going platforms, often pitching and rolling, and were required to halt within a couple of hundred feet.

Left: Our distinguished contributor Rear-Admiral Ray Rawbone—here a Lieutenant—climbs aboard his Seafire III, HMS *Stalker*, 1945. The photograph offers a detailed view of the FAA's flying appurtenances of the day: flying gloves (in the left hand), helmet and goggles, earphones, Pusser's wristwatch, oxygen mask slung beneath the chin and, of course, the trusty Mae West lifejacket. The parachute can be seen inside the cockpit.

Below: Personnel of 809 Squadron on board *Stalker* in the Far East, off Trincomalee in the summer of 1945: (front row, left to right) the CBAL (Carrier-Borne Army Liaison officer, name unknown), unknown, Sub-Lieutenants John Brittain, David Lees-Jones and Little, Lieutenant Ray Rawbone (SP), Lieutenant-Commander Andrew Bloomer (CO), Sub-Lieutenants Fry, James, Davi(e)s and Morrison, unknown and unknown; (back row, left to right) Sub-Lieutenant Morris, next four unknown, Sub-Lieutenants Herring, Mant and Holmes, and last four unknown. Notice the Seafire III's wing-fold jury struts and the asymmetrical positioning of the wing roundels.

816 NAVAL AIR SQUADRON

Located at RNAS Machrihanish and Maydown and RCAF Argenta and on board HMS *Tracker*.

Commission: 01/02/42–01/08/44 (Seafire Mk IICs 00/06/43–00/08/43, Seafire Mk IBs 00/08/43–00/12/43)
Commanding Officers: Lt-Cdr P. F. Pryor, Lt-Cdr F. C. Nottingham DSC (12/07/43)
Senior Pilots: Not known

FRONT-LINE SEAFIRE SQUADRONS

833 NAVAL AIR SQUADRON   *Believed no crest authorised*

Located at RNAS Machrihanish and on board HMS *Stalker*.

Commission: 08/12/41–07/01/44 (Seafire Mk IICs 00/06/43–00/09/43)
Commanding Officer: Lt-Cdr J. R. C. Callander
Senior Pilots: Not known

834 NAVAL AIR SQUADRON

Located at RNAS Machrihanish, RAF Santa Cruz and RNAS Puttlam and Katukurunda and on board HM Ships *Hunter* and *Battler*.

Commission: 12/11/41–06/12/44 (Seafire Mk IICs 00/06/43–11/08/44)
Commanding Officer: Lt-Cdr E. D. Child
Senior Pilots: Not known

Left: One of the small number of 'composite' squadrons flying Seafires for air defence duties in conjunction with Swordfish A/S aircraft, 834 was the only unit to operate as such in the Indian Ocean, on board HMS *Battler*. In this somewhat truncated photograph, Seafire Mk IIC LR7?2/'Z' flies in company with two of the Squadron's Swordfish.

842 NAVAL AIR SQUADRON

Located at RNAS Machrihanish and Belfast and at Lagens (Azores) and on board HMS *Fencer*.

Commission: 01/03/43–15/01/45 (Seafire Mk IBs 00/07/43–26/03/44, Mk IICs 00/07/43–00/08/43)
Commanding Officer: Lt-Cdr L. R. Tivy
Senior Pilots: Not known

Left: 842 Squadron, another Swordfish anti-submarine unit, had a Seafire flight for almost twelve months, and the aircraft were flown regularly during HMS *Fencer*'s Atlantic duties. Here a collapsed undercarriage leg has caused problems for a returning pilot.
Below: Another Seafire lands on board *Fencer*, 'bouncing' while, thankfully, managing to hold on to the arrester wire. The raised safety barrier, the last line of defence for aircraft parked forward, is clearly seen.

879 NAVAL AIR SQUADRON

Located at RNAS Stretton, Machrihanish, Burscough, Long Kesh, Dekheila, Katukurunda, Trincomalee, Nutts Corner *et alibi* and on board HMS *Attacker*.

Commission: 30/09/42-07/01/46 (Spitfire Mk VAs/VBs/VBs Hooked 00/03/43-00/03/43, Seafire Mk IBs 00/03/43-00/06/43, Mk IICs 00/06/43-00/11/45, Mk IIIs 00/03/44-00/11/45, Mk XVIIs 00/11/45-07/01/46)
Commanding Officers: Lt-Cdr R. J. H. Grose RNVR, Lt-Cdr P. E. I. Bailey (09/11/44), Lt-Cdr B. H. Harriss (14/04/45)
Senior Pilots: Not known

Left: 879 Squadron, which was commissioned as a sort of offshoot of 809 Squadron, was in effect the sea-going equivalent of an army co-operation unit, spending a good deal of its period of service in support of land forces operating around the Mediterranean from on board HMS *Attacker*, either as a single unit or as small detachments of aircraft sent at short notice to deal with specific problems. This Seafire IIC of the Squadron suffered serious front-end damage when it crash-landed on board ship on 9 September 1943. Its serial number is not known, but it carries the intriguing code characters '?' and 'Q' either side of the roundel, their red finish hardly distinguishable against the camouflaged paintwork in this monochrome photograph.

880 NAVAL AIR SQUADRON

Located at RAF North Front, RNAS Machrihanish, Stretton, Skeabrae, Grimsetter and Jervis Bay, RAAF Schofields *et alibi* and on board HM Ships *Argus*, *Indomitable*, *Furious* and *Implacable*.

Commission: 15/01/41-11/09/45 (Spitfire Is/VBs 00/08/42-00/01/44), Seafire Mk IICs 00/09/42-00/03/44, Mk IIIs 00/03/44-11/09/45)
Commanding Officers: Lt-Cdr R. J. Cork DSO DFC, Lt-Cdr W. H. Martyn DSC RNVR (07/09/42), Lt-Cdr R. M. Crosley DSC* RNVR (04/08/44)
Senior Pilots: Not known

Left: 880 NAS was equipped with Seafires from 1942 until its de-commissioning, progressing from Mk IICs to Mk IIIs in the spring of 1944. Here a disabled Mk IIC from the Squadron is manhandled on deck following a landing mishap. The code letters are very prominent, by virtue of having been outlined in white paint.

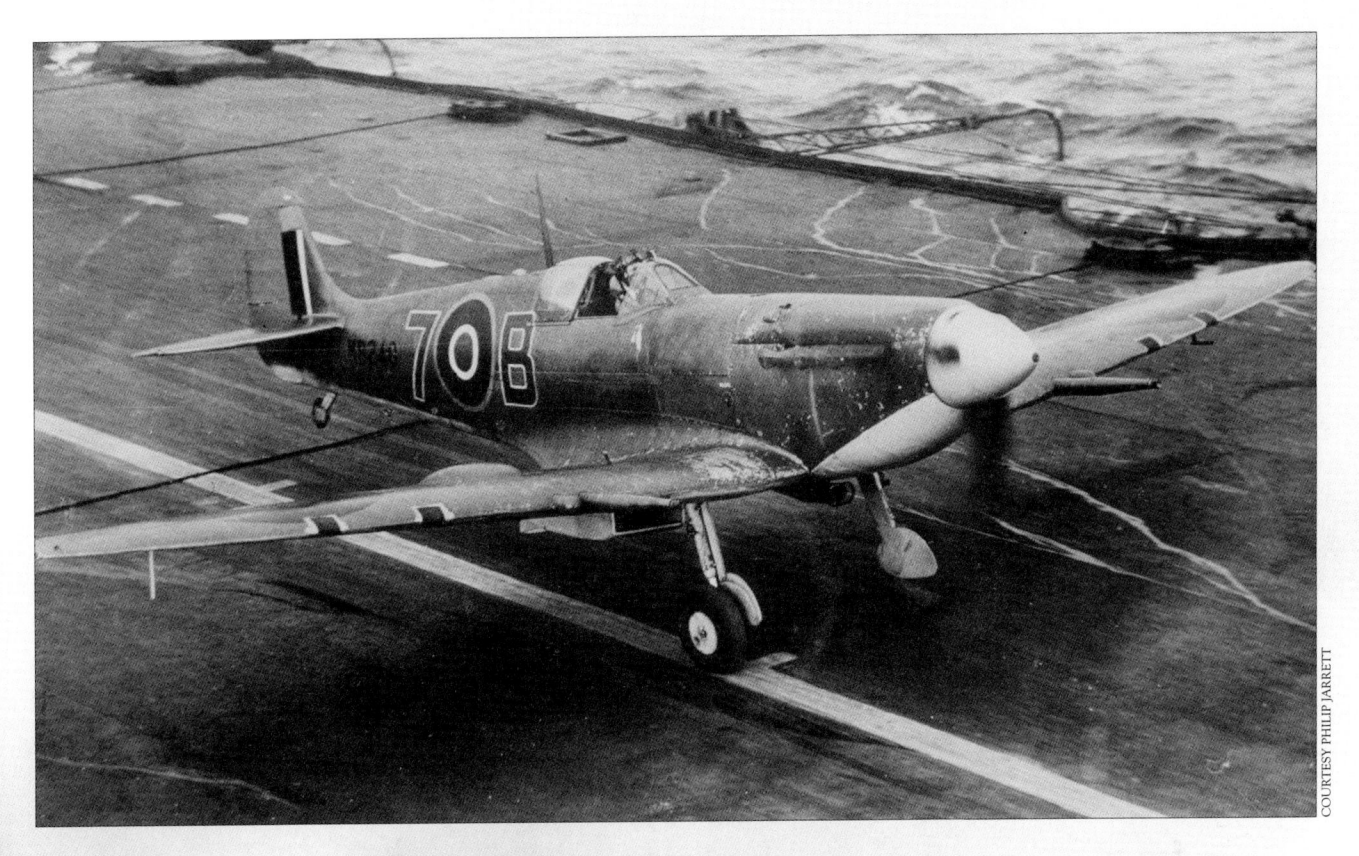

Above: Seafire MB240, a Mk IIC from 880 Squadron, makes a free take-off from HMS *Indomitable*, There is much chipping of paintwork around the engine covers, and notice, too, that the machine-gun ports have been sealed off with taped canvas patches—probably painted red—to prevent the ingestion of general detritus.
Below: Another photograph from on board *Indomitable*, summer 1943, and here the errant tailwheel and the raised arrester hook suggest that the pilot is carrying out a 'touch-and-go' landing. This Seafire, another Mk IIC, is MB253 and is coded '7R'. Summer 1943. One interesting point about this photograph is that it illustrates a 'wrinkle' specific to these early Seafires. It was of course the practice for pilots to slide back their cockpit canopies when taking off or landing on board carriers, in order to facilitate egress or rescue if anything went wrong, but an additional trick—seen here—was to open the cockpit door just a fraction, keeping it 'on the latch': this prevented the canopy from sliding forward, which it inevitably would otherwise have done during the sudden and rapid deceleration brought about by the arrest. It also ensured that the canopy remained open if the pilot was unfortunate enough to go overboard into 'the drink'.

883 NAVAL AIR SQUADRON

Located at RNAS Arbroath, Nutts Corner and Machrihanish; and at NAS Dartmouth and on board HMS *Magnificent*.

Commissions: 18/09/45-23/02/46, 15/05/47-01/05/51 (Seafire Mk IIIs 18/09/45-00/11/45, Mk XVs 00/11/45-23/02/46 and 15/05/47-00/09/48)
Commanding Officers: Lt-Cdr T. J. A. King-Joyce, Lt-Cdr R. A. Monks RCN (15/05/47), Lt-Cdr J. B. Fotheringham RCN (00/01/48)
Senior Pilots: Not known

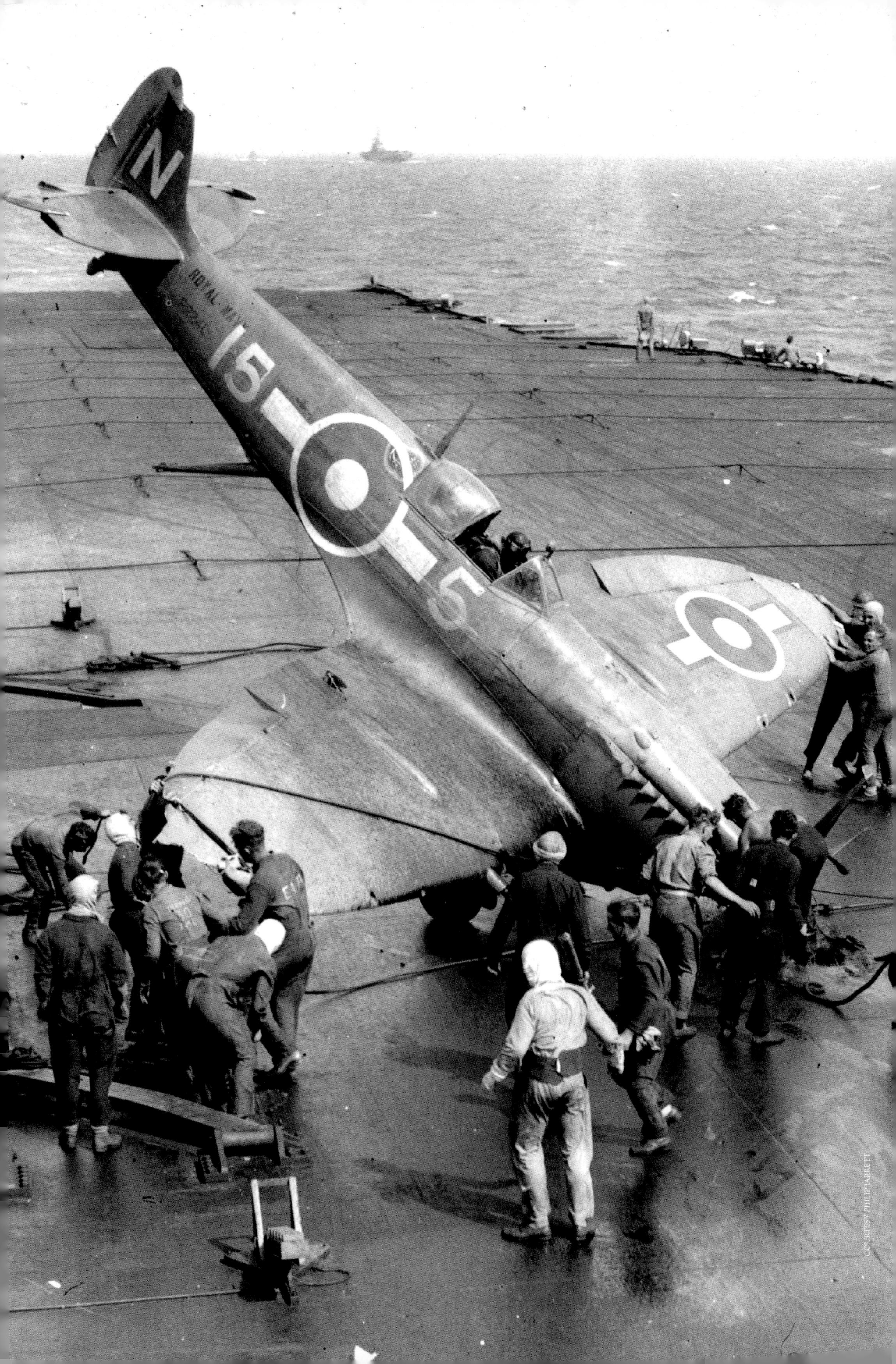

COURTESY PHILIP JARRETT

FRONT-LINE SEAFIRE SQUADRONS

884 NAVAL AIR SQUADRON

Located at RNAS Skeabrae and Grimsetter, RAF Turnhouse and Drem and RNAS Machrihanish.

Commission: 01/11/41-20/07/43 (Spitfire Mk VAs/VBs/VBs Hooked 00/09/42-00/10/42, Seafire Mk IICs 00/09/42-20/07/43)
Commanding Officers: Lt-Cdr N. G. Hallett, Lt-Cdr T. B. Winstanley (20/03/43)
Senior Pilots: Not known

885 NAVAL AIR SQUADRON

Located at RNAS Machrihanish, RAF North Front and Ta Kali and RNAS Lee-on-Solent, St Merryn, Henstridge *et alibi* and on board HMS *Formidable*.

Commission: 01/12/41-15/11/43, 15/02/44-27/09/45 (Spitfire Mk VAs/VBs/VBs Hooked 00/09/42-00/10/42, Seafire Mk IICs 00/09/42-00/11/43, Mk IBs 00/10/42-00/08/43, Mk IIIs 00/02/44-00/11/44)
Commanding Officers: Lt-Cdr R. H. P Carver DSC, Lt-Cdr S. L. Devonald (15/02/44)
Senior Pilots: Not known

886 NAVAL AIR SQUADRON

Located at RAF Turnhouse and Peterhead, RNAS Stretton and Machrihanish, RAF North Front, RNAS Burscough, Lee-on-Solent and Henstridge, RAF Ayr *et alibi* and on board HMS *Attacker*.

Commission: 15/03/42-19/07/44 (Spitfire Mk VBs/VBs Hooked 00/02/43-00/03/43 and 00/02/44-00/03/44, Seafire Mk IICs 00/03/43-00/02/44, Spitfire Mk XIIIs (sic) 00/03/44-00/03/44, Seafire Mk IIIs 00/03/44-19/07/44)
Commanding Officers: Lt-Cdr R. H. H. L. Oliphant RNVR, Lt-Cdr P. E. I. Bailey (28/10/43)
Senior Pilots: Not known

Left: Seafire Mk III PR240 of 880 Squadron after engaging the safety barrier on board *Implacable*, June 1945, during operations off Truk by the British Pacific Fleet. The pilot is apparently none the worse for the experience: nobody is taking an interest in him, for sure.

Below: A famous Seafire image: a Mk IIC of 885 Squadron (*Formidable*, during Operation 'Torch') running up its engine prior to take-off with matelots at the wing tips and a pair on the tailplane to steady things. It was not unknown for aircraft to take to the air with a body clinging to the tail!

COURTESY PHILIP JARRETT

111

887 NAVAL AIR SQUADRON

Located at RNAS Lee-on-Solent, Machrihanish, St Merryn, Henstridge, Burscough, Eglinton, Skeabrae and Katukurunda, RAAF Schofields *et alibi* and on board HMS *Indefatigable*.

Commission: 01/05/42–15/03/46 (Spitfire Mk VAs 00/12/42–00/02/43, Seafire Mk IBs 00/02/43–00/03/43, Mk IICs 00/03/43–00/12/43, Mk IIIs 00/12/43–00/03/46)
Commanding Officers: Lt-Cdr D. W. Kirke, Lt-Cdr B. F. Wiggington DSC RNVR (04/01/44), Lt-Cdr A. J. Thomson DSC RNVR (19/08/44), Lt-Cdr N. G. Hallett DSC** (14/05/45), Lt-Cdr G. Dennison RNVR (27/09/45)
Senior Pilots: Not known

Above: 887 Squadron pilots photographed while serving on board HMS *Unicorn* in the early summer of 1943: (left to right) Sub-Lieutenants Chipps (possibly a nickname), Dave Olds, Des Viney and Harry Foote, Lieutenant Bill Daubney, Lieutenant-Commander David Kirke (CO), Sub-Lieutenants Jack Basley, Bill Coleman and 'Duke' Beever, Petty Officer Pilot Buck Taylor, Lieutenant (?) Pete Knowler and Sub-Lieutenant Tony King.

Below: Heart in mouth: LR817, an 887 Squadron Seafire Mk III, strays perilously close to the edge of *Unicorn*'s flight deck—so close, in fact, that the barrier stanchion is in the process of being demolished by the propeller. The accident was probably the result of an off-centreline landing, and possibly carried out at too high a speed.

FRONT-LINE SEAFIRE SQUADRONS

Above: Rain-soaked flight decks were hated by aircrews and handling crews alike, for they significantly increased the risk of accidents. Here an 887 Squadron pilot awaits clearance to proceed in his Seafire III across just such a hazardous surface.

Left, upper: A 'floater'—a landing aircraft that refuses to make contact with the flight deck—was a common sight, and here the aftermost of the two safety barriers on board HMS *Indefatigable* has been rigged so as to act as an additional arrester wire. Everybody will be hoping that this Seafire III's hook will snag this 'last chance' device. 887 Squadron, summer 1944.

Left, lower: 'Bats' beats a hasty retreat from his platform as a Seafire III of 887 Squadron slides into the port catwalk on board HMS *Implacable*. This incident occurred after the war.

889 NAVAL AIR SQUADRON *Believed no crest authorised*

Located at RNAS Colombo Racecourse and Puttalam and on board HMS *Atheling*.

Commission: 01/04/44–11/07/44 (Seafire Mk IICs and IIIs throughout)
Commanding Officers: Lt-Cdr F. A. J. Pennington RNZVR, Lt-Cdr J. B. Edmundson (24/04/44), Lt-Cdr D. A. E. Holbrook (11/06/44)
Senior Pilots: Not known

894 NAVAL AIR SQUADRON

Located at RNAS Hatston, RAF North Front, RNAS Henstridge, Burscough, Ballyhalbert, Eglinton, Lee-on-Solent and Katukurunda, RAAF Schofields *et alibi* and on board HMS *Indefatigable*.

Commission: 15/08/42-15/03/46 (Seafire Mk IBs 00/02/43-00/03/43, Spitfire Mk VBs 00/03/43-00/04/43, Seafire Mk IICs 00/03/43-00/11/43, Mk IIIs 00/11/43-15/03/46)
Commanding Officers: Lt-Cdr D. A. van Epps RNVR, Lt-Cdr F. R. A. Turnbull DSC (17/06/43), Lt-Cdr C. Walker (17/01/44), Lt-Cdr J. Crossman DSO RNVR (18/07/44), Lt-Cdr J. R. Routley RNVR (24/10/45), Lt-Cdr R. M. Crosley DSC* RNVR (07/01/46)
Senior Pilots: Not known

Above: NN460/'H6-Z' of 894 Squadron makes contact with the barrier on board HMS *Indefatigable*, January 1945; the starboard main undercarriage leg is severely buckled and the propeller has started to disintegrate. When aircraft were moved from European to Far East operations, the order to modify the national insignia was interpreted in various ways. It can be seen that this aircraft's fuselage roundel is in miniature, and lacks the broad bars either side that other units favoured (as seen in other photographs in this book). The vital element in the process was the removal of all traces of red paint, although this modification does not appear yet to have been applied to the fin flash in this instance.

895 NAVAL AIR SQUADRON

Located at RNAS St Merryn and Machrihanish and RAF Turnhouse.

Commission: 15/11/42-30/06/43 (Seafire Mk IICs 00/03/43-30/06/43)
Commanding Officer: Lt-Cdr J. W. Hedges RNVR
Senior Pilot: Not known

897 NAVAL AIR SQUADRON

Located at RNAS Lee-on-Solent, St Merryn, Machrihanish, Burscough, Henstridge *et alibi* and on board HM Ships *Unicorn* and *Stalker*.

Commission: 01/12/42-15/07/44 (Spitfire Mk VBs/VBs Hooked 00/03/43-00/12/43 and 00/03/44-15/07/44, Seafire Mk IBs 00/03/43-00/07/43, Mk IICs 00/08/43-00/05/44)
Commanding Officer: Lt-Cdr W. C. Simpson DSC
Senior Pilots: Not known

899 NAVAL AIR SQUADRON

Located at RNAS Lee-on-Solent, St Merryn, Machrihanish, Burscough, Henstridge *et alibi* and on board HM Ships *Unicorn* and *Stalker*.

Commission: 01/12/42–15/07/44 (Spitfire Mk VBs/VBs Hooked 00/03/43–00/12/43 and 00/03/44–15/07/44, Seafire Mk IBs 00/03/43–00/07/43, Mk IICs 00/08/43–00/05/44)
Commanding Officer: Lt-Cdr W. C. Simpson DSC
Senior Pilots: Not known

Above: NN344 'K-O' of 899 Squadron lands on board the escort carrier HMS *Khedive* and draws to a halt as a crewman at the deck-edge indicates that the safety barrier can be collapsed as it is now not required. The photograph was taken during Operation 'Dragoon' in the summer of 1944.

Below: Clouds of powder issue from hand-held fire extinguishers as rescue crews attend an 899 Squadron Seafire in trouble after landing on board *Khedive*. There was always the danger of a sudden conflagration—one good reason why pilots making an approach kept their cockpit canopies open.

RNVR SEAFIRE SQUADRONS

THE end of World War II initiated large-scale decommissioning amongst Fleet Air Arm squadrons and the disposal of a large number of aircraft, resulting in the rapid disappearance from the inventory of Merlin-engined Seafires. The Griffon-engined marks were still under development, however, and Mk XVs and XVIIs continued to be issued to a limited number of front-line units. The ultimate Seafire, the Mk 47, was introduced into service in 1948, but already its successor, the more capable Hawker Sea Fury, was beginning to take its place, while the XV and XVII—by now referred to using arabic numerals—continued to form the backbone of the FAA's fighter training units.

For the Royal Naval Volunteer Reserve, however, the Seafire was the equipment of choice when, in the summer of 1947, its Air Branch began to take up its duties: 1830 at RNAS Abbotsinch received a small number of Mk 17s (discarded when it was decided that the Squadron would concentrate on anti-submarine activities with its Fireflies); 1831 at Stretton was issued with Mk 17s; 1832, based at RNAS Culham, received a mixture of Mk 15s and 17s; and 1833 at Bramcote commissioned with Mk 17s. In due course 1832 took delivery of a small number of Mk 46s and in 1950, to the considerable envy of the other RNVR units, 1833 re-equipped with contra-prop Mk 47s as these became surplus to the requirements of the front line. Seafires were finally withdrawn from the RNVR, in favour of the Sea Fury, in May 1954, by which time they had all but disappeared from second-line squadrons too.

Left: Seafires of 1832 Squadron at Culham, with Seafire Mk 46 LA561 in the foreground and Mk 17s beyond.
Above: RNVR Seafires at sea on board the reserve and training carrier HMS *Illustrious* in September 1950. Such embarkations permitted the 'Weekend Warriors' to hone their skills in the finer arts of naval aviation.
Below: Much activity as 1832 Squadron prepare for flying at Culham. Seafire 17s are being checked and refuelled, and pilots are starting their engines.

1830 NAVAL AIR SQUADRON

Located at RNAS Abbotsinch.

Commission: 15/08/47–10/03/57 (Seafire Mk 17s 15/08/47–00/05/48)
Commanding Officer: Lt-Cdr J. D. Murricane DSC RNVR
Senior Pilots: Not known

1831 NAVAL AIR SQUADRON

Located at RNAS Stretton.

Commission: 01/06/47–10/03/57 (Seafire Mk 15s 01/06/47–00/08/51, Mk 17s 01/06/47–00/08/51)
Commanding Officers: Lt-Cdr H. G. Mitchell DSC RNVR, Lt-Cdr R. I. Gilchrist MBE RNVR (26/05/48)
Senior Pilots: Not known

1832 NAVAL AIR SQUADRON

Located at RNAS Culham.

Commission: 01/07/47–10/03/57 (Seafire Mk IIIs 01/07/47–00/11/47, Mk 46s 00/08/47–00/01/50, Mk 17s 00/06/48–00/05/53, Mk 15s 00/04/49–00/08/51)
Commanding Officers: Lt-Cdr P. Godfrey OBE RNVR, Lt-Cdr G. M. Rutherford MBE DSC RNVR (01/02/52), Lt-Cdr G. R. Willcocks DSC RNVR (01/06/52)
Senior Pilots: Not known

Below: During the RNVR's annual training, those squadrons embarked continued to uphold the Seafire's reputation as a tricky aircraft to deck-land. This Mk 17 from 1831 Squadron, SX242, 'pranged' on board *Illustrious* on 6 September 1950 when it bounced over the wires.
Opposite, top: An airborne trio of 1831 Squadron Seafire 17s, still wearing their camouflaged paintwork of the immediate postwar period. The Stretton tail code, 'JA', was changed to the more logical 'ST' in 1953.
Opposite, centre: A 1832 Squadron Mk 17 photographed in 1952. The aircraft lacks a side number but sports a 'clockwork mouse' emblem on the engine casing, implying a specific rôle associated with Aerodrome Dummy Deck Landings (ADDLs): it is possible that this *décor* was inherited from a spell of duty SX194 enjoyed with 767 Squadron, the dedicated ADDL training unit.
Opposite, bottom: LA555, a Seafire Mk 46 from 1833 Squadron, touches down at Culham. The paint finish accords with the standard postwar FAA disruptive camouflage scheme.

RNVR SEAFIRE SQUADRONS

Above: SX311, one of 1833 Squadron's Seafire Mk 17s, runs up its engine prior to a take-off during DLT on board HMS *Triumph* in June 1952. The propeller spinner is painted red.

Right and below: Further scenes from Culham: Seafire Mk 46s and, more distantly, Mk 17s receive attention; and, in the lower photograph, Squadron officers pose for a quick photograph. The Mk 46s—and indeed other Seafires of the era—are often described as wearing homogeneous Extra Dark Sea Grey paintwork on their uppersurfaces but in fact they wore disruptive camouflage, the other shade being Dark Slate Grey. In monochrome photographs, the two colours are exceedingly difficult to distinguish.

1833 NAVAL AIR SQUADRON

Located at RNAS Bramcote.

Commission: 15/08/47–10/03/57 (Seafire Mk XVIIs 15/08/47–00/07/52, Mk XVs 00/07/49–00/08/51, Mk 47s 00/06/52–00/05/54)
Commanding Officers: Lt-Cdr L. F. Auckland DSC RNVR, Lt-Cdr R. I. M. Scott OBE RNVR (16/03/48), Lt-Cdr R. F. Hallam RNVR, Lt-Cdr B. W. Vigrass RNVR (01/04/52)
Senior Pilots: Not known

Above: The Bramcote-based 1833 Squadron received the potent Seafire Mk 47 in July 1952—the only RNVR unit to do so. This example, VP442, is seen wearing temporary red and yellow wing and fuselage bands. The aircraft is equipped for the fighter-reconnaissance rôle, with camera ports behind and below the cockpit on either side of the fuselage, and has vacant rocket rails beneath its wings.

Below: Forlorn and abandoned, 1833 Squadron Mk 47s await their inevitable fate following the disbandment of the RNVR in 1957.

SECOND-LINE SEAFIRE SQUADRONS

SEAFIRES equipped an exceedingly large number of the Fleet Air Arm's second-line units, which from 1942 were kept busy evaluating the aircraft as it progressed from the standard RAF Spitfire, training hundreds of sorely needed fighter pilots and providing the support necessary to ensure that the maximum benefit was derived from the design. These duties continued, with considerably smaller numbers of aircraft, of course, after the war. The tables in this section list the squadrons involved, together with their base stations, marks of Seafire flown, commanding officers and summarised rôle.

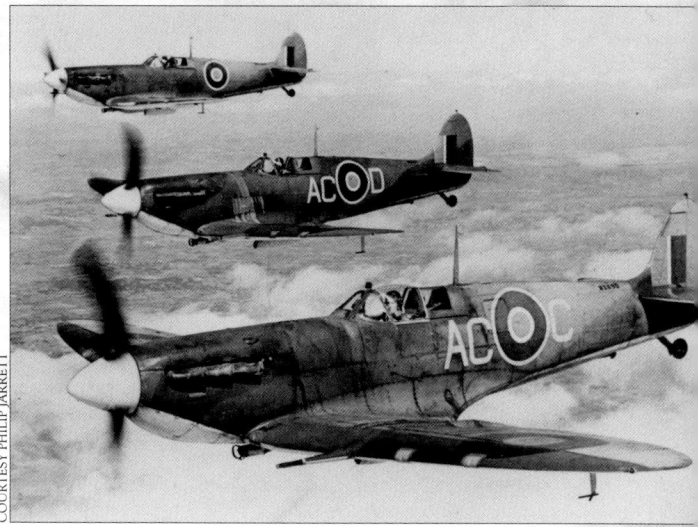

Unit	Location(s)	Commission(s)
700 NAS	RNAS Yeovilton (1948-49) and Ford (1955-56)	11/10/44-30/09/49 (Seafire Mk IBs 00/09/45-00/12/45, Mk IICs 00/11/45-00/12/45, Mk IIIs 00/02/45-00/02/46, Mk XVs 00/02/45-00/03/49)
703 NAS	RAF Thorney Island and RNAS Lee-on-Solent	19/04/45-17/08/55 (Seafire Mk XVIIs 00/00/47-00/08/49, 1 × Mk 45 00/12/45-00/00/46)
706 NAS	RAAF Schofields, RNAS Nowra *et alibi*	06/03/45-31/05/46 (Seafire Mk IIIs 06/03/45-00/11/45, Mk XVs 00/00/46-31/05/46)
708 NAS	RNAS Gosport	01/10/44-26/02/46 (Seafire Mk IBs 00/05/45-00/06/45, Mk IICs 00/05/45-00/06/45, Mk IIIs 00/05/45-00/08/45)
709 NAS	RNAS St Merryn	15/09/44-06/01/46 (Seafire Mk IIIs 15/09/44-00/08/45, Mk XVs 00/11/45-06/01/46, 1 × Mk 45 00/00/45-06/06/46)
715 NAS	RNAS St Merryn	17/08/44-31/03/46 (Seafire Mk IBs 17/08/44-00/00/45, Mk IIIs 17/08/45-00/12/45, Mk XVIIs 17/08/44-00/12/45)
718 NAS	RNAS Henstridge, Ballyhalbert and Eglinton	05/06/44-01/11/45 (Seafire Mk IIIs and Spitfire Mk XIIIs throughout, Seafire Mk ICs 00/07/44-31/10/45) and 23/08/46-17/03/47 (Seafire Mk IIIs 23/08/46-00/09/46, Mk XVs 00/00/46-17/03/47)
719 NAS	RNAS St Merryn	15/05/44-02/01/45 (Spitfire Mk VBs/VBs Hooked and Seafire Mk IBs and IICs throughout)
721 NAS	Archerfield (Australia) and RAF Kai Tak	01/03/45-21/11/47 (Seafire Mk IIIs 00/00/46-21/11/47, Mk XVs 00/11/46-21/11/47)
727 NAS	RNAS Gosport	23/04/46-17/01/50 (1 × Seafire Mk XVII 23/04/46-00/02/47)
728 NAS	RAF Luqa and RNAS Hal Far	08/05/43-31/05/67 (Seafire Mk IICs 00/01/45-00/01/46, Mk IIIs 00/07/45-00/07/46, Mk XVs 00/09/46-00/09/48, Mk XVIIs 00/05/48-00/06/52)

Opposite page, far left: Seafire XV PR419 of 790 Squadron at Culdrose, having veered from the runway and nosed over. The aircraft wears the rarely seen 'DL' (for RNAS Dale) tail code.
Left: A well-known Seafire photograph showing Mk IBs of 736 Squadron based at St Merryn during the war. The nearest aircraft is NX890 and the next in the formation is NX924. These aircraft were originally built as Spitfire Mk VBs for the Royal Air Force, which explains the positions of the serial numbers: traces of the original 'BL'-prefixed RAF serials, in the standard position, are still discernible on NX890 and on the third Seafire.
Above: Seafire Mk 17 SX369 serving with the Naval Air Fighter School (736, 738 and, from 1951, 759 Squadrons) at Culdrose in 1950 or 1951 and apparently sporting a replacement rudder in dark finish.

Commanding Officer(s)	Remarks
Lt-Cdr L. R. E. Castlemaine RNVR, Cdr P. H. C. Illingworth (20/05/46), Lt-Cdr G. F. Hawkes (02/02/48), Lt R. M. Orr-Ewing (03/05/48), Lt W. J. Lovell (18/02/49)	Maintenance Test Pilot Training Squadron (50th Air Training Group 1948–49).
Lt-Cdr J. H. Dundas DSC, Lt-Cdr J. C. N. Shrubsole DSC (25/04/47), Lt-Cdr W. R. J. McWhirter DSC (22/04/48)	Naval Air–Sea Warfare Development Unit; from 1948, Service Trials Unit.
Lt-Cdr R. E. Bradshaw DSC**, Lt-Cdr D. M. R. Wynne-Roberts (31/08/45)	Aircrew pool and refresher training for British Pacific Fleet.
Lt K. White MBE, Lt D. L. R. Hutchinson DSC RNVR (20/08/45)	Tactical trials unit for Blackburn Firebrand (Seafires employed as comparative/adversarial aircraft).
Cdr W. C. Simpson DSC RNVR, Lt-Cdr D. B. Law DSC (05/01/46)	Ground Attack School (part of School of Naval Air Warfare).
Lt-Cdr R. E. Gardner DSC RNVR, Lt-Cdr D. G. Carlisle DSC SANF(V) (12/12/44), Lt-Cdr F. R. A. Turnbull DSC* (28/06/45)	Fighter air combat and Fighter Leader training.
Lt-Cdr W. H. Stevens, Lt-Cdr S. J. Hall DSC (26/11/44), Lt-Cdr R. M. Crosley DSC* (23/08/46), Lt A. C. Lindsay DSC (13/11/46)	Army Co-operation Naval Operational Training Unit; from 1945, School of Air Reconnaissance; from 23/08/46, Seafire conversion unit.
Lt-Cdr J. L. Appleby	Air Firing Training unit. Absorbed by 794 NAS (q.v.) on disbandment.
Lt-Cdr F. A. Simpson RNVR, Lt-Cdr J. L. Moore (07/03/46), Lt-Cdr R. D. Head DSC* (19/11/46)	Fleet requirements unit (Pacific theatre).
Lt A. M. Dennis, Lt R. B Lunberg (10/01/47)	Training unit for Air Courses.
Lt-Cdr P. B. Pratt RNVR, Lt-Cdr E. M. Britton (05/01/46), Lt P. J. W. W. Cruttenden RNVR (03/06/46), Lt J. R. W. Groves (21/10/46), Lt-Cdr D. H. Lough (14/10/48), Lt-Cdr R. P. Keogh (06/10/49), Lt-Cdr H. A. Monk DSC (12/10/50), Lt-Cdr P. C. S. Bagley (04/02/52)	Fleet requirements unit.

continued . . .

Squadron	Base	Dates
731 NAS	RNAS East Haven	05/12/43-01/11/45 (Seafire Mk IBs 00/05/44-00/02/45, Mk IICs 00/00/45-00/11/45)
733 NAS	RNAS Trincomalee	01/01/44-31/12/47 (Seafire Mk IIIs 00/10/46-00/12/46, Mk XVs 00/01/47-31/12/47)
736 NAS	RNAS Yeovilton, St Merryn and Culdrose	24/05/43-26/03/65 (Seafire Mk IBs 24/05/43-00/08/44, Mk IIIs 00/08/44-00/02/46, Spitfire Mk VAs 00/03/44-00/08/44, Seafire Mk XVIIs 00/01/46-00/04/51, Mk 46s 00/01/46-00/12/46, Mk XVs 00/04/46-00/06/48)
737 NAS	RNAS Eglinton	30/03/49-22/11/57 (Seafire Mk XVs 00/04/49-00/01/50, Mk XVIIs 00/04/49-00/05/50)
738 NAS	RNAS Culdrose	01/05/50-08/05/70 (Seafire Mk XVIIs 01/05/50-00/09/51, Mk 46s 01/05/50-00/08/50)
740 NAS	RNAS Machrihanish	30/12/43-01/09/45 (Seafire Mk IIIs 00/07/45-01/09/45)
741 NAS	RNAS St Merryn	12/08/46-25/11/47 (Seafire Mk IIIs 00/02/47-25/11/47)
744 NAS	RNAS Eglinton	06/03/44-01/12/47 (Seafire Mk IIIs 00/05/46-00/00/47)
746 NAS	RAF West Raynham and RNAS Hatston	23/11/42-30/01/46 (Seafire Mk XVIIs 00/12/45-30/01/46)
748 NAS	RNAS St Merryn, Yeovilton, Henstridge and Dale	12/10/42-11/02/46 (Spitfire Mk Is 12/10/42-00/04/43, Mk VAs 00/02/43-00/07/44, Seafire Mk IBs 00/06/43-11/02/46, Mk IICs 00/03/43-11/02/46, Spitfire Mk VBs Hooked 00/03/45-11/02/46, Seafire Mk IIIs 00/11/45-11/02/46)
751 NAS	RAF Watton	01/03/47-30/09/47 (Seafire Mk XVs 00/07/47-30/09/47)
757 NAS	RNAS Puttalam	02/10/43-29/01/46 (Seafire Mk IICs 00/06/44-00/00/45, Mk IIIs 00/05/45-29/01/46)
759 NAS	RNAS Yeovilton, Zeals and Culdrose	01/11/39-05/02/46 (Spitfire Mk Is 00/06/40-00/08/44, Mk Vs 00/05/43-00/10/44, Mk IIs 00/08/43-00/10/43, Seafire Mk IBs 00/08/43-00/01/45, Mk IICs 00/05/44-00/02/45, Mk IIIs 00/12/45-05/02/46, Mk XVs 00/00/45-05/02/46) and 16/08/51-12/10/54 (Seafire Mk XVIIs 16/08/51-00/07/54, Mk 47s 00/09/52-00/11/53)
760 NAS	RNAS Zeals, Lee-on-Solent and Henstridge	21/04/45-23/01/46 (Seafire Mk IIIs 00/10/45-23/01/46)
761 NAS	RNAS Henstridge	01/08/41-16/01/46 (Spitfire Mk Is 00/09/42-00/07/44, Mk VAs/VBs/VBs Hooked 00/04/43-00/02/45, Seafire Mk IBs 00/04/43-00/03/45, Mk IICs 00/07/44-00/08/45, Mk IIIs 00/04/44-16/01/46, Mk XVs 00/07/45-16/01/46, Mk XVIIs 00/11/45-16/01/46)
762 NAS	RNAS Yeovilton	23/03/42-09/06/43 (Spitfire Mk Is 00/02/43-09/06/43)
764 NAS	RNAS Gosport	08/04/40-01/09/45 (Seafire Mk XVIIs 00/00/45-00/08/45)
766 NAS	RNAS Lossiemouth	15/04/42-25/11/54 (Seafire Mk IIIs 00/08/46-00/09/47, Mk XVs 00/06/47-00/11/51, Mk XVIIs 00/07/47-00/11/52)
767 NAS	RNAS East Haven, Milltown, Yeovilton and Henstridge	24/05/49-31/03/55 (Seafire Mk IIIs 00/03/46-00/06/47, Mk XVs 00/05/46-00/02/52, Mk 46s 00/03/50-00/07/50)
768 NAS	RNAS Arbroath, Machrihanish, Ayr, Abbotsinch, Ballyhalbert, East Haven and Eglinton	13/01/41-16/04/46 (Spitfire Mk VAs/VBs Hooked 00/10/42-00/02/45, Seafire Mk IBs 00/07/43-00/02/45, Mk IICs 00/01/44-16/04/46, Mk IIIs 00/06/44-16/04/46) and 15/12/48-08/03/49 (Seafire Mk XVs throughout)
770 NAS	RNAS Crail and Dunino and RAF Drem	07/11/39-01/10/45 (Seafire Mk IICs 00/09/43-01/10/45, Spitfire Mk Vs 00/05/45-00/07/45)
771 NAS	RNAS Gosport and Lee-on-Solent	01/08/45-06/10/47 (Seafire Mk IIIs 00/03/46-00/01/47, Mk XVs 00/11/46-00/01/51, Mk 45s 00/12/47-00/09/50, Mk 46s 00/05/47-00/12/47)
772 NAS	RNAS Burscough and Anthorn	28/09/39-13/10/48 (Seafire Mk IIIs 00/03/46-00/08/46)

Lt-Cdr K. Stilliard RNVR, Lt-Cdr R. Pridham-Wippel (01/01/45)	Deck Landing Control Officer ('batsman') training.
Lt-Cdr H. J. Mortimore	Fleet requirements unit.
Lt-Cdr R. E. Gardiner DSC RNVR, Lt-Cdr D. R. Curry DSC (17/08/44), Lt-Cdr P. D. Gick (08/02/45), Lt-Cdr S. P. Luke (03/08/45), Lt-Cdr D. B. Law DSC (06/01/46), Lt-Cdr W. Stuart DSC RNVR (16/04/46), Lt-Cdr J. G. Baldwin DSC (24/04/47), Lt-Cdr M. F. Fell DSO DSC (21/10/47), Lt-Cdr P. J. P. Leckie (05/09/49), Lt-Cdr P. B. Stuart (01/02/50), Lt-Cdr P. M. Austin (17/10/50), Lt-Cdr P. H. London DSC (24/03/52)	School of Air Combat; from 1950, Naval Air Fighter School (flying training). 'B' Flight, extant 01/03/45–26/09/45, formed by redesignating 'Y' Flight of 767 NAS (q.v.).
Lt-Cdr J. L. Appleby, Lt-Cdr W. C. Simpson DSC (10/05/49), Lt-Cdr A. Turnbull (15/12/49)	Operational Flying School Part II.
Lt-Cdr S. F. F. Shotton, Lt-Cdr S. A. Mearns DSC (19/01/51), Lt-Cdr H. J. Abraham (12/07/51)	Naval Air Fighter School (weapons training).
Lt-Cdr L. T. Summerfield RNVR	Communications unit.
Lt-Cdr S. G. Cooper, Lt-Cdr T. W. Harrington DSC* (25/08/47)	Operational Flying School Part II.
Lt R. H. W. Blake	Anti-submarine training.
Lt-Cdr G. L. C. Davies DSC	Naval Night Fighter Development Squadron.
Lt-Cdr R. G. French RNVR, Lt-Cdr B. H. C. Nation (05/11/43), Lt-Cdr J. G. Smith RNVR (20/07/44), Lt-Cdr P. J. E. Nichols RNVR (05/08/45), Lt-Cdr P. C. S. Chilton (17/12/45)	Refresher flying for fighter pilots.
Lt R. J. F. Forty	Radar trials unit.
Lt-Cdr G. W. Parrish DSC RNVR, Lt-Cdr R. W. Durrant DSC RNZNVR (05/05/45), Lt-Cdr F. W. Baring RNVR (24/11/45)	Operational training unit and pool for fighter pilots.
Lt-Cdr B. H. M. Kendall, Lt-Cdr H. P. Bramwell DSO DSC (18/11/40), Capt. F. D. G. Bird RM (01/08/41), Lt-Cdr J. N. Garnett (13/10/41), Lt-Cdr E. W. T. Taylour DSC (08/12/41), Lt-Cdr E. D. G. Lewin DSO DSC (12/11/42), Lt-Cdr J. M. Bruen DSO DSC (07/12/42), Lt-Cdr N. G. Hallett DSC (17/05/43), Maj. F. D. G. Bird RM (20/12/43), Lt-Cdr O. N. Bailey (10/07/44), Lt-Cdr J. W. Sleigh DSO DSC (14/12/44), Lt-Cdr R. D. Lygo (16/08/51), Lt-Cdr D. R. O. Price (30/05/53)	Fleet Fighter School; from 1943, Advanced Flying School; from 1951, No 1 Operational Flying School.
Lt-Cdr R. Tebble	Element of No 1 Naval Fighter School.
Lt-Cdr R. J. Cork DSO DSC (10/04/43), Lt-Cdr R. H. P. Carver DSC (15/11/43), Lt-Cdr S. G. Orr DSC RNVR (20/09/44), Lt-Cdr P. N. Charlton DFC (27/04/45)	Fleet Fighter School Advanced Training Squadron; from 1943, No 2 Naval Air Fighter School.
Lt D. B. M Fiddes, Lt-Cdr M. J. S. Newman (29/03/43)	Advanced flying training.
Lt G. A. Donaghue RNVR, Capt D. B. L. Smith RM (03/06/45)	User trials unit.
Maj. V. B. G. Cheesman MBE DSO DSC RM, Lt-Cdr T. W. Harrington DSC* (01/12/47), Lt-Cdr A. W. Bloomer (30/03/49), Lt-Cdr J. M. Henry (21/01/51), Lt-Cdr D. W. Winterton (02/12/52)	Operational Flying School Part I.
Lt-Cdr F. A. Swanton DSC*, Lt J. C. S. Wright (26/08/46), Lt-Cdr L. D. Empson (24/11/46), Lt-Cdr J. S. Toner (14/01/49), Lt P. H. Mogridge DSC (27/04/49), Lt-Cdr W. E. Simpson (29/11/49), Lt-Cdr C. K. Roberts (19/04/50), Lt M. E. Stanley (18/01/51), Lt-Cdr D. o'D. Newberry (03/09/51)	Deck landing training and Deck Landing Control Officer ('batsman') training.
Lt P. B. Jackson, Lt-Cdr D. M. Brown RNVR (29/12/42), Lt-Cdr D. J. W. Williams (01/03/43), Lt-Cdr J. S. Bailey (08/07/43), Lt-Cdr J. M. Brown DSC RNVR (29/10/44), Lt-Cdr R. Pridham-Wippel (01/11/45), Lt N. A. Bartlett (10/01/46), Lt D. G. MacQueen MBE	Deck landing training unit; from 1948 Deck Landing Officer ('batsman') re-training (for changeover to US Navy signalling system).
Lt-Cdr A. F. E. Payne RNVR, Lt-Cdr D. R. M. Manthorpe RNVR (05/04/44), Lt-Cdr J. M. L. Wilson RNZNVR (13/08/45)	Fleet requirements unit.
Lt-Cdr G. M. T. Osborn DSO DSC, Lt-Cdr C. R. Bateman (23/02/48), Lt-Cdr R. W. M. Walsh (07/01/49), Lt-Cdr J. G. Baldwin DSC (18/11/49), Lt-Cdr J. A. Welply (18/12/50)	Fleet requirements unit.
Lt-Cdr P. Snow	Fleet requirements unit.

continued ...

Left: Seafire Mk XVII SX273 of 741 Squadron up from St Merryn and showing a rare dash of colour in the form of spinner, ailerons, wing tips and stabilisers painted, it is believed, yellow and matching the hue of the code letters. 741 was affiliated to the Naval Air Fighter School and specialised in air-to-air combat training.

773 NAS	RNAS Lee-on-Solent and RAF North Front and on board HM Ships *Implacable* and *Vengeance*		04/01/50–31/03/50 (Seafire Mk XVs throughout)
775 NAS	RNAS Dekheila and RAF North Front		00/11/40–00/03/46 (Spitfire Mk Is/VCs 00/00/43–00/00/43, Seafire Mk IICs 00/08/44–00/11/45)
776 NAS	RNAS Woodvale and Burscough		10/01/41–30/10/45 (Seafire Mk IICs 00/05/45–30/10/45)
777 NAS	RNAS Gosport and Ayr and on board HMS *Pretoria Castle*		23/05/45–03/01/46 (Seafire Mk XVs 00/05/45–00/07/45, Mk XVIIs 00/12/45–00/03/46, Mk 45s 00/05/45–00/06/45, Mk 46s 00/00/45–00/01/46)
778 NAS	RNAS Arbroath, Crail, Gosport, Ford and Lee-on-Solent and RAF Tangmere		28/09/39–16/08/48 (Spitfire Mk VBs 00/00/41–00/00/41, Mk XIIs 00/02/43–00/03/43, Mk IXs 00/04/44–00/05/45, Seafire Mk IBs 00/01/42–00/01/45, Mk IICs 00/07/42–00/04/44, Mk IIIs 00/06/43–00/03/47, Mk XVs 00/03/44–00/08/46, Mk XVIIs 00/07/45–00/07/48, Mk 45s 00/06/45–00/10/47, Mk 46s 00/07/46–00/01/48, Mk 47s 00/12/46–00/03/47)
779 NAS	RAF North Front		01/10/41–05/08/45 (Seafire Mk IBs 00/05/43–00/10/44, Mk IIIs 00/05/45–00/08/45)
780 NAS	RNAS Hinstock, Crail and Donibristle		28/03/46–16/11/49 (Seafire Mk XVs 00/07/46–00/10/46, Mk 45s 00/11/46–00/00/47)
781 NAS	RNAS Lee-on-Solent		20/03/40–31/07/45 (Seafire Mk IBs 00/07/43–31/07/45, Mk IIIs 00/08/44–31/07/45) and 27/06/46–31/03/81 (Mk 15s 00/12/49–00/02/50, Mk 17s 00/05/49–00/10/49, Mk 46s 00/03/47–00/00/47)
782 NAS	RNAS Donibristle		23/09/40–09/10/53 (Seafire Mk IIIs 00/05/47–00/01/48, Mk XVIIs 00/12/47–00/10/48)
787 NAS	RAF Duxford, Wittering, Tangmere, Westhampnett and West Raynham		05/03/41–16/01/56 (Seafire Mk IBs 00/07/42–00/08/44, Mk IICs 00/11/42–00/03/45, Mk IIIs 00/12/43–00/06/46, Mk XVs 00/09/44–00/06/46, Mk XVIIs 00/04/45–00/02/48, Mk 45s 00/03/46–00/02/48, Mk 47s 00/05/47–00/09/49)
790 NAS	RNAS Zeals, Dale and Culdrose		27/07/42–15/11/49 (Spitfire Mk VBs 00/02/45–00/00/47, Seafire Mk IBs 00/03/45–00/00/47, Mk IICs 00/03/45–00/00/47, Mk IIIs 00/11/46–00/02/47, Mk XVs 00/05/47–00/01/49)
791 NAS	RNAS Arbroath		19/10/40–10/12/44 (Spitfire Mk Is 00/10/42–00/05/43)
794 NAS	RNAS Yeovilton, Angle, Dale, Henstridge, Charlton Horethorne and (from 1945) Eglinton		03/08/40–30/06/44 (Spitfire Mk Is/VAs/VBs 00/09/42–00/00/44, Mk VBs Hooked 00/11/43–30/06/44) and 02/01/45–26/02/47 (Spitfire Mk VBs Hooked 02/01/45–00/05/45, Seafire Mk IICs 00/02/45–00/00/46, Mk IIIs 00/06/46–26/02/47)
798 NAS	RNAS Lee-on-Solent		11/10/43–18/03/46 (Spitfire Mk VBs/IXs 00/12/44–00/06/45, Seafire Mk IBs 00/06/45–00/07/45, Mk IICs 00/06/45–00/00/45)
799 NAS	RNAS Lee-on-Solent, Yeovilton and Machrihanish		30/07/45–12/08/52 (Seafire Mk IICs 00/08/45–00/07/47, Mk IIIs 00/08/45–00/07/47, Mk XVs 00/10/45–00/11/51, Mk XVIIs 00/12/47–00/06/52)

Right: PR317, coded 'IT-3C', of 767 Squadron, having met with a nasty accident whilst employed in deck landing training with OFS Part I at Milltown, probably on board HMS *Vengeance*, March 1947. The aircraft, a Seafire XV, is in the process of being recovered.

Lt-Cdr R. C. B. Trelawney	Fleet requirements unit (for Home Fleet's 1950 Spring Cruise).
Lt-Cdr J. M. Waddell RNVR, Lt-Cdr J. L. Wordsworth RNVR (24/03/45)	Fleet requirements unit with fighter flight.
Lt-Cdr N. G. MacLean RNVR	Fleet requirements unit.
Lt D. R. Carter RNVR, Lt-Cdr J. R. N. Gardner (04/06/45)	Trials unit.
Lt-Cdr A. J. Tillard, Lt-Cdr H. P. Bramwell DSO DSC (21/07/41), Lt-Cdr H. J. F. Lane (01/03/43), Lt-Cdr P. B. Schonfield (25/04/44), Lt-Cdr E. M. Britton (05/02/45), Lt-Cdr M. A. Lacayo (01/10/45), Lt-Cdr R. H. P. Carver DSC (03/07/46), Lt-Cdr F. R. A. Turnbull DSC* (16/01/48)	Service Trials Unit/Carrier Trials Unit.
Lt-Cdr C. R. Holman RNR, Lt-Cdr E. L. Meiklejohn RNVR (14/098/43)	Fleet requirements unit.
Lt D. C. E. F. Gibson DSC, Lt W. E. Cotton (17/12/46)	Advanced flying training unit and Naval Instrument Flying School.
Lt-Cdr Sir George J. E. Lewis Bt RNVR, Lt-Cdr W. B. Caldwell RNVR (01/12/44), Lt-Cdr P. F. Clayton (19/08/46), Lt L. W. A. Barrington (07/07/48)	Communications unit (Southern Communications Squadron).
Lt-Cdr T. E. Sargent	Communications unit (Flag Officer Flying Training duties).
Cdr B. H. M. Kendall OBE, Cdr R. A. Kilroy DSC 06/05/46), Lt-Cdr P. E. I. Bailey (03/12/46), Cdr R. J. H. Stephens (11/02/47), Cdr E. A. Shaw (21/04/48)	Naval Air Fighting Development Unit/Air Fighting Development Squadron. 'Y' Flight (Seafire Mk IBs/IICs/IIIs) at RNAS Arbroath, Burscough et alibi 00/06/44–01/03/45.
Lt-Cdr G. K. Pridham RNVR, Lt-Cdr R. Williams RNVR (23/04/45), Lt-Cdr M. J. A. O'Sullivan (16/11/45), Lt-Cdr H. Muir-Mackenzie (15/06/47), Lt-Cdr B. Sinclair MBE (14/08/48)	Fighter Direction Officer training.
Lt J. C. M. Harman, Lt-Cdr C. A. Crighton RNVR (12/05/43)	Target-towing unit.
Lt-Cdr F. C. Muir RNVR, Lt W. H. Stevens (16/11/42), Lt-Cdr A. L. Hill RNVR (10/04/43), Lt-Cdr T. L. Crookston (06/01/44), Lt-Cdr J. L. Appleby (02/01/45), Lt-Cdr R. A. Bird DSC (03/07/45), Lt-Cdr G. Dennison RNVR (11/04/46), Lt A. C. Lindsay DSC (01/08/46), Lt-Cdr R. M. Crosley DSC* (13/11/46)	Target-towing duties; from 1945, School of Air Firing.
Lt-Cdr I. J. Wallace OBE RNVR, Lt-Cdr S. W. Birse DSC RNR (08/08/45)	Advanced conversion and refresher flying.
Lt-Cdr T. E. Sargent RNR, Lt-Cdr N. R. Quill RNR (04/01/46), Lt-Cdr P. W. Compton DSC (04/11/46), Lt-Cdr J. B. Harrowar DSC RNVR (01/07/47), Lt-Cdr J. N. Ball DSC (16/01/48), Lt T. J. Harris (13/05/48), Lt J. D. Nunn (28/10/48), Lt K. G. Talbot (06/06/49), Lt-Cdr G. R. Callingham (26/04/50), Lt-Cdr B. H. Harriss (01/03/51), Lt-Cdr G. F. Birch (12/11/51)	Flying Check and Refresher Conversion Squadron; from 1951, Refresher Flying Training Unit.

SEAFIRE

Left, upper: Seafire miscellany—1. The only known use of a Seafire as a gate guardian was at RNAS Culdrose in the mid-1950s. However, its presence there was short-lived, the principal reason for its removal being that, as the aircraft's propeller could spin freely and its wing-tip navigation lights could function, uninformed passing motorists imagined that they were about to witness a crash-landing!

Left, lower: Seafire miscellany—2. The only preserved Seafire Mk 47 is VP441, shown here at Culdrose in 1965. The aircraft—ex 804 Squadron—was transferred to Squires Gate Airport Museum in Blackpool in 1970 but fell derelict when this establishment went out of business, after which it was bought by an American collector, who restored it and returned it to flying condition. It now resides in Texas, registered as NX47SF. It was announced on 1 July 2010 that a Mk 15, PR503, had taken to the air that day in Missouri after a protracted period of restoration, bring the total number of airworthy Seafires to three (all of which are Griffon-powered).

Below: The Fleet Air Arm Museum's static Seafire exhibit, SX137. It is a Mk 17.

SEAFIRE COLOURS

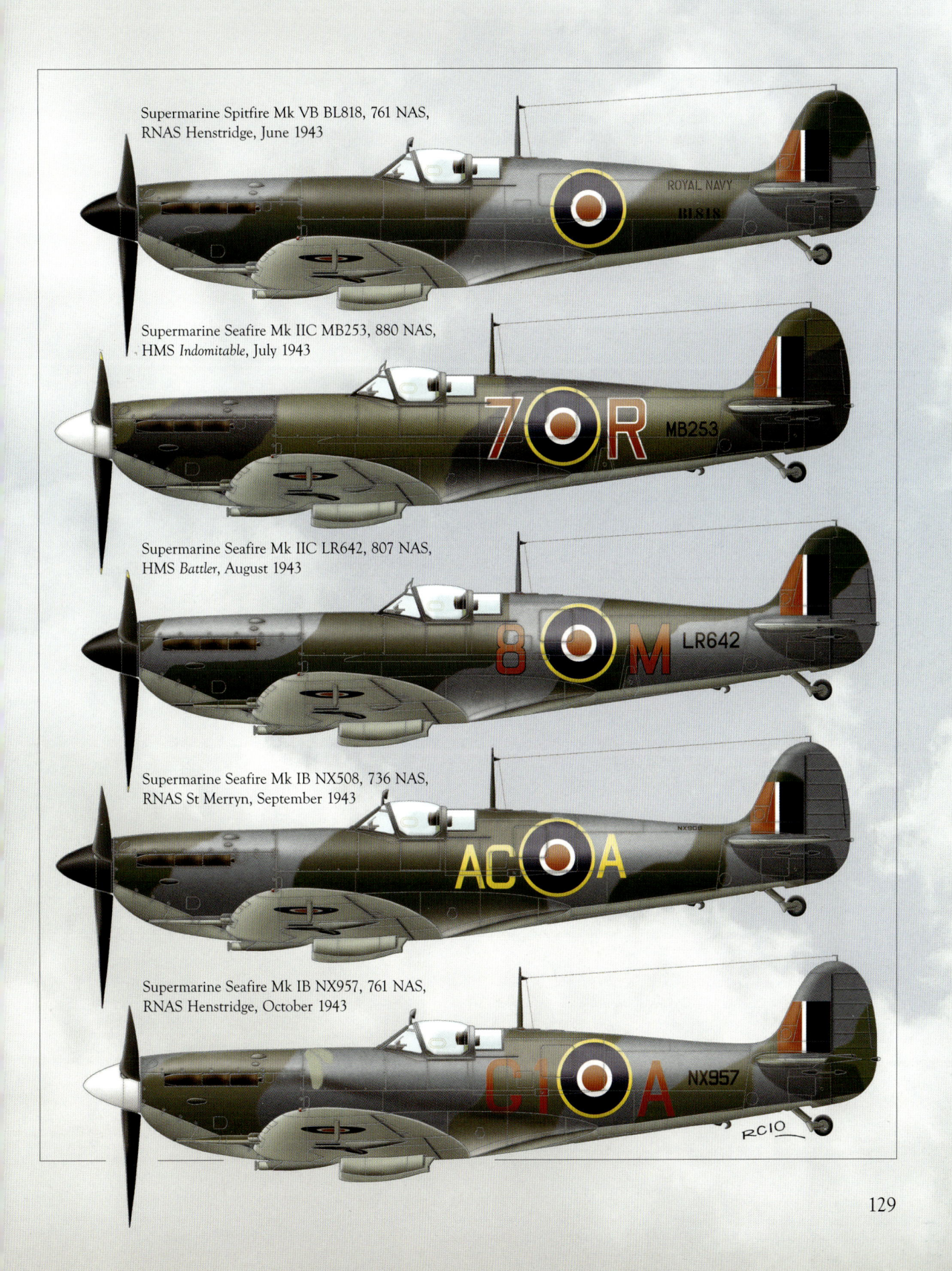

Supermarine Spitfire Mk VB BL818, 761 NAS,
RNAS Henstridge, June 1943

Supermarine Seafire Mk IIC MB253, 880 NAS,
HMS *Indomitable*, July 1943

Supermarine Seafire Mk IIC LR642, 807 NAS,
HMS *Battler*, August 1943

Supermarine Seafire Mk IB NX508, 736 NAS,
RNAS St Merryn, September 1943

Supermarine Seafire Mk IB NX957, 761 NAS,
RNAS Henstridge, October 1943

129

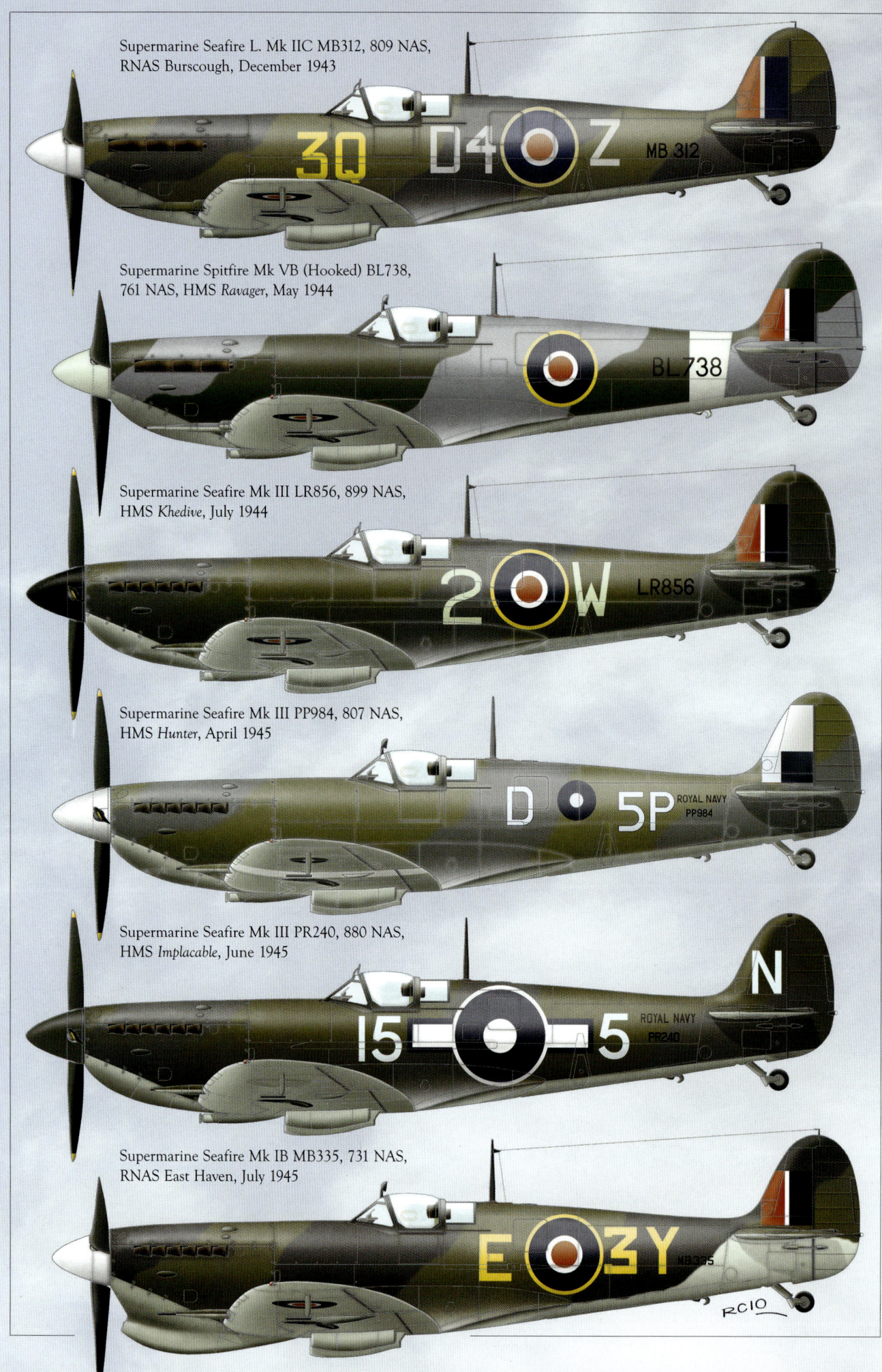

SEAFIRE

Supermarine Seafire L. Mk IIC MB312, 809 NAS,
RNAS Burscough, December 1943

Supermarine Spitfire Mk VB (Hooked) BL738,
761 NAS, HMS *Ravager*, May 1944

Supermarine Seafire Mk III LR856, 899 NAS,
HMS *Khedive*, July 1944

Supermarine Seafire Mk III PP984, 807 NAS,
HMS *Hunter*, April 1945

Supermarine Seafire Mk III PR240, 880 NAS,
HMS *Implacable*, June 1945

Supermarine Seafire Mk IB MB335, 731 NAS,
RNAS East Haven, July 1945

SEAFIRE COLOURS

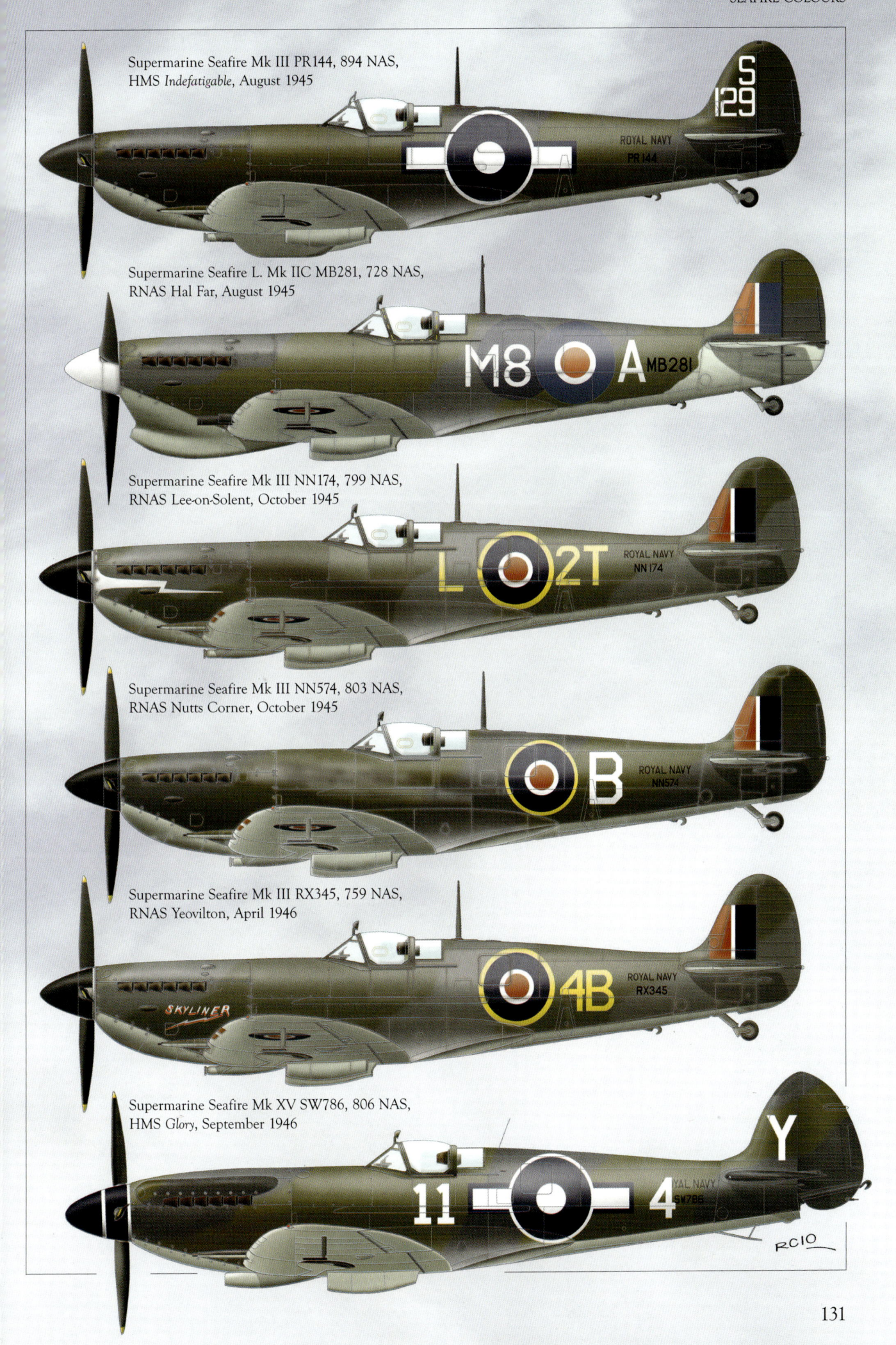

Supermarine Seafire Mk III PR144, 894 NAS,
HMS *Indefatigable*, August 1945

Supermarine Seafire L. Mk IIC MB281, 728 NAS,
RNAS Hal Far, August 1945

Supermarine Seafire Mk III NN174, 799 NAS,
RNAS Lee-on-Solent, October 1945

Supermarine Seafire Mk III NN574, 803 NAS,
RNAS Nutts Corner, October 1945

Supermarine Seafire Mk III RX345, 759 NAS,
RNAS Yeovilton, April 1946

Supermarine Seafire Mk XV SW786, 806 NAS,
HMS *Glory*, September 1946

131

# FLOWN BY THE AUTHOR

SEAFIRE COLOURS

SUPERMARINE SEAFIRE F Mk XV
NS490 (second prototype), RAE Farnborough, July 1944

133

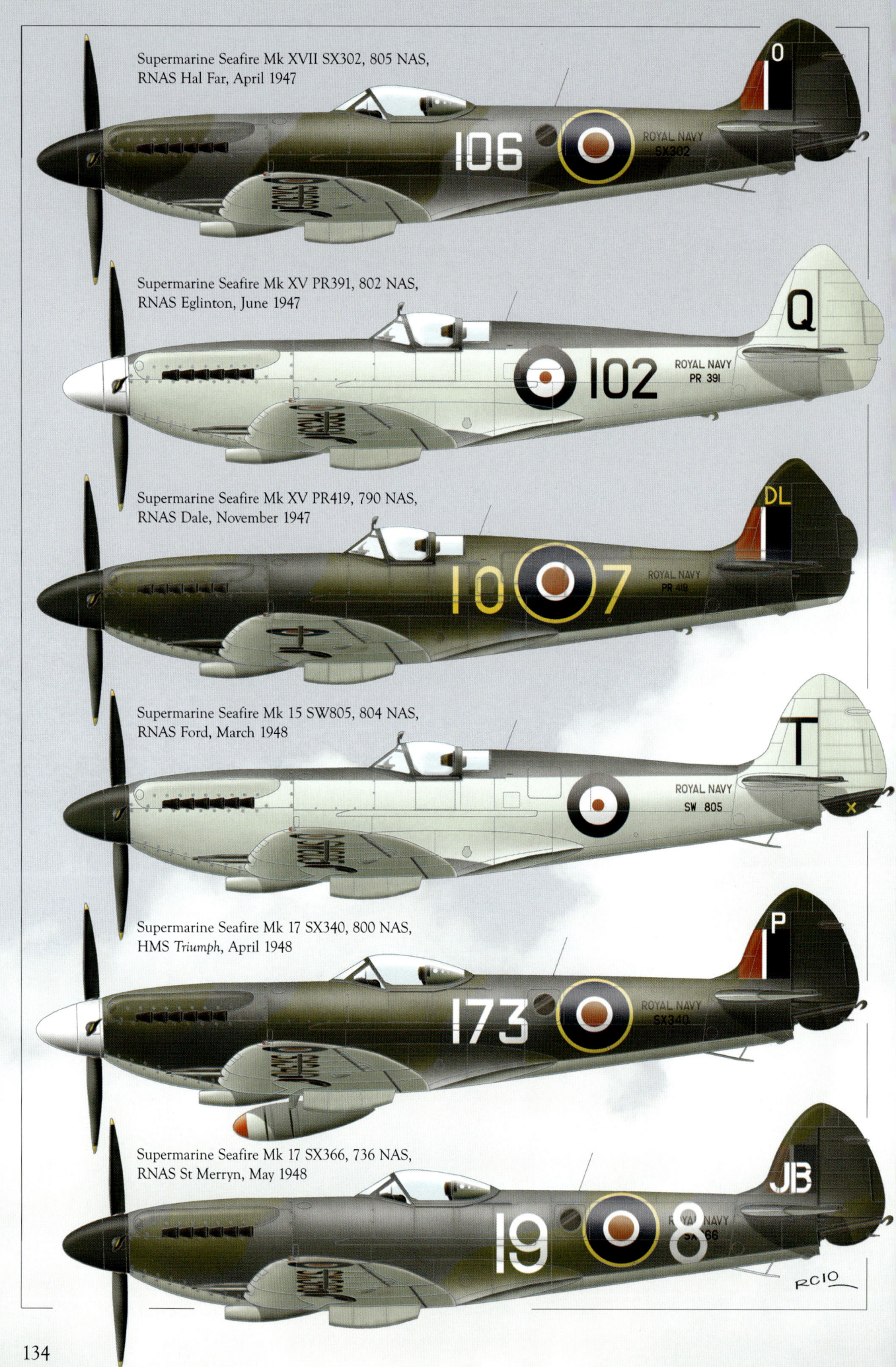

SEAFIRE

Supermarine Seafire Mk XVII SX302, 805 NAS,
RNAS Hal Far, April 1947

Supermarine Seafire Mk XV PR391, 802 NAS,
RNAS Eglinton, June 1947

Supermarine Seafire Mk XV PR419, 790 NAS,
RNAS Dale, November 1947

Supermarine Seafire Mk 15 SW805, 804 NAS,
RNAS Ford, March 1948

Supermarine Seafire Mk 17 SX340, 800 NAS,
HMS *Triumph*, April 1948

Supermarine Seafire Mk 17 SX366, 736 NAS,
RNAS St Merryn, May 1948

134

SEAFIRE COLOURS

Supermarine Seafire Mk 46 LA555, 1832 NAS,
RNAS Culham, May 1948

Supermarine Seafire Mk 45 LA496, 771 NAS,
RNAS Lee-on-Solent, September 1948

Supermarine Seafire Mk 47 VP458, 804 NAS,
HMS *Ocean*, April 1949

Supermarine Seafire Mk 15 SW910, 1832
NAS, RNAS Culham, August 1949

Supermarine Seafire Mk 17 SP343, 1832 NAS,
RNAS Culham, January 1950

Supermarine Seafire Mk 17 SX122, 1831 NAS,
RNAS Stretton March 1950

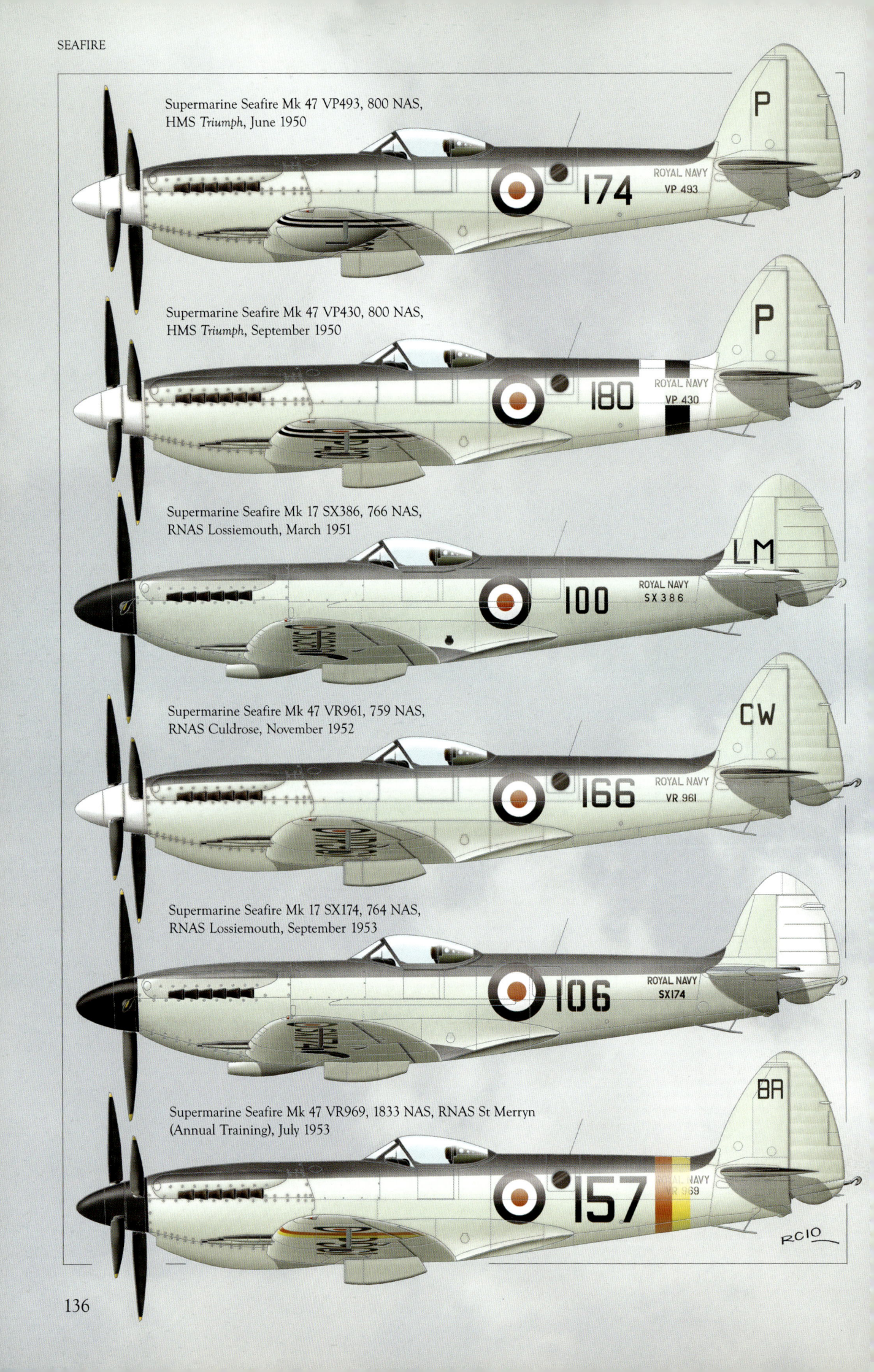

SEAFIRE

Supermarine Seafire Mk 47 VP493, 800 NAS,
HMS *Triumph*, June 1950

Supermarine Seafire Mk 47 VP430, 800 NAS,
HMS *Triumph*, September 1950

Supermarine Seafire Mk 17 SX386, 766 NAS,
RNAS Lossiemouth, March 1951

Supermarine Seafire Mk 47 VR961, 759 NAS,
RNAS Culdrose, November 1952

Supermarine Seafire Mk 17 SX174, 764 NAS,
RNAS Lossiemouth, September 1953

Supermarine Seafire Mk 47 VR969, 1833 NAS, RNAS St Merryn
(Annual Training), July 1953